bible and ethics in the christian life

bible and ethics in the christian life

+

BRUCE C. BIRCH
LARRY L. RASMUSSEN

AUGSBURG PUBLISHING HOUSE
MINNEAPOLIS, MINNESOTA

BIBLE AND ETHICS IN THE CHRISTIAN LIFE

MANUFACTURED IN THE UNITED STATES OF AMERICA

contents

To the
students, faculty, and staff
of
Wesley Theological Seminary

preface

A book is a joint venture. The contributions are never the author's alone. This book is no exception. In a variety of ways many friends have given their skills to this volume. While we are, of course, responsible for the final outcome, our efforts were supported in collegial fashion. Dr. J. Philip Wogaman, Dean, Wesley Theological Seminary, and Dr. James Childress, Center for Bioethics, Kennedy Institute, Georgetown University, supplied a careful reading of the manuscript. If the final draft is an improved one, it is because of their insight and conversation. Dr. Francine Jo Cardman, Assistant Professor of Church History, Wesley Theological Seminary, gave equally valuable criticism for the redraft of chapter four. The authors whose work is reviewed in chapter two all gave of their time to check the accuracy of our presentation. David Earle Anderson, Religion Editor, United Press International, provided helpful editorial suggestions. Judith Birch, Dorothy Briggs, Virginia Hamner, Pat Hayden, and Carolyn Schneider made possible the meeting of deadlines for the typed manuscript. James McGinnis prepared the bibliography.

This book is a joint venture in still another way. It began as a result of a teaching effort together, a seminar entitled "Bible and Ethics." Our earliest discovery was the paucity of materials that addressed the task we had put before the seminar, to make the connections between biblical materials and those in current Christian ethics in a way that does justice to both. The weekly struggles of the seminar only confirmed the need to construct a framework for functionally relating Bible and ethics. The students of that seminar deserve special thanks for their major role in the formation of this volume. Two colleagues in the respective fields, Dr. Brevard S. Childs, Professor of Old Testament, Yale University, and Dr. James M. Gustafson, University Professor of Theological Ethics, University of Chicago, also merit special mention. Our thinking has been greatly stimulated by their thoughtful deliberations.

The dedication of this volume to the students, faculty, and staff of Wesley Theological Seminary further underscores this book as a joint venture. They are the community in which we work. That the work is challenging and enjoyable, even in critical times in this city, is their doing.

BRUCE C. BIRCH
LARRY L. RASMUSSEN

Washington, D.C.

introduction

Morality and ethics have always been regarded as central to the Christian life. The Christian community has always struggled with the kinds of persons Christians should be and the actions they should take. It has always sought faithful response to God in day-to-day affairs and it has endeavored to shape life in keeping with what ought to be.

The Bible has always been regarded as central for Christian morality and ethics. It has, in fact, been regarded as the charter document for the Christian moral life. Biblical materials have been enlisted again and again for the fashioning of character and conduct. They have been consulted repeatedly for guidance and authority. Every generation has drawn lines between its own moral wrestlings and those of the biblical communities. The scriptures have been a seminal source and resource for the moral life.

Two fields of study, Christian ethics and biblical studies, have a special charge in theological education and within Christian reflection generally. They are called on most directly to aid the Christian and the church in making that essential connection

11

between the primal documents of the faith—the scriptures—and the faith's daily expression in the moral life. Students of both fields have always rightly and readily asserted the importance of each to the other for the living out of the Christian life and for the ongoing life of the church.

Yet there has been a striking and marked divergence of these particular fields. Christian ethics and biblical studies as arenas of scholarship have lost touch with one another. Brevard Childs reports with full accuracy in his *Biblical Theology in Crisis:*

> . . . In spite of the great interest in ethics, to our knowledge, there is no outstanding modern work written in English that even attempts to deal adequately with the Biblical material as it relates to ethics.[1]

What has happened? Perhaps sheer complexity. The knowledge explosion and the growing intricacy and sophistication of many sciences has meant a lengthy and increasingly specialized education for students in each of these fields. The generalist has been replaced by the specialist. The result is that only rarely is the ethicist now competent as a biblical scholar or the biblical scholar sophisticated as an ethicist.

It is time to make the connections between these fields and to assist in the functional relating of Bible and ethics in the Christian life. This volume has that as its purpose. It attempts to begin "dealing adequately with the biblical material as it relates to ethics." Undertaking that in a single volume means imposing certain limits, to be sure, especially in light of the fact that the last century of unparalleled work has vastly altered the terrain in biblical studies, and the same century has seen unprecedented change challenge Christian ethics at every point. Still, a core set of questions presents itself and these questions can be addressed within the scope of these pages.

What kind of authority for Christian morality is the Bible?

At what points and for what purposes in the Christian moral life might biblical materials have an appropriate and influential role?

How do the different types of biblical materials function in the moral life? How are they made available and properly used?

What are the tasks of Christian ethics and at what critical points does Christian ethics draw on biblical materials? For what purposes?

What role does the church play in the relating of the Bible and Christian ethics?

We want, then, to address a set of questions around the Bible's use and authority in the Christian moral life and to do so in a way that helps bridge the gap between two fields of study vital to the life of the church.

1 the divergence of biblical studies and christian ethics

What has been the relationship of Christian ethics to biblical studies? And in the world of biblical scholarship what has been addressed to Christian ethics? An overview of the relationship of each field to the other is critical to the later discussions. Notice must also be given the way in which relationships between these two fields have been reflected in the life of the church.

Christian Ethics and the Bible

Childs' remark about the absence of materials relating the Bible and ethics was made from the side of biblical scholarship. It holds equally well, however, from the side of Christian ethics. James Gustafson reported in his widely applauded survey:

> In spite of the great interest in ethics in the past thirty years, and in spite of the extensive growth of biblical studies, there is a paucity of material that relates the two areas in a scholarly way. Writers in ethics necessarily make their forays into the Bible without the technical exegetical and historical acumen and skills to be se-

cure in the way they use biblical materials. But few biblical scholars have provided studies upon which writers
in ethics can draw.[1]

Thus for Christian ethics, too, there is no "outstanding modern
work . . . in English that even attempts to deal adequately with
the biblical material as it relates to ethics" (Childs).

This curious and lamentable state of affairs is sometimes recognized for the deformation it is. Charles Curran's survey of the
use of the Bible in Roman Catholic writings begins with the
noteworthy acknowledgment:

> . . . The contemporary moral theologian has rejected
> the moral manuals of the past for many reasons, but the
> failure to find a basic orientation and grounding in the
> Scriptures frequently is mentioned as a most important
> lack in the older textbooks.[2]

Curran's reference is to moral theology before Vatican II. Yet
the judgment of Brevard Childs is also borne out for more recent
Roman Catholic works, as we shall soon see.

The case with Protestant writings is somewhat different. They
have often used biblical materials heavily, attempting the "basic
orientation and grounding in the Scriptures" Curran notes as a
stark shortcoming in Catholic writings. The Protestant materials
have suffered a different omission, the omission of a *methodological self-consciousness* that would press the vital question
whether the biblical materials have been dealt with *adequately*
as they relate to ethics. The judgments of Childs and Gustafson
hold for both Protestant and Catholic ethics.

If the deformation were confined to the well-paneled chambers
of scholars, the damage would be slight. But the impact is more
wide-spread. Leander Keck and James Sellers portray this graph-

ically in the case study of their seminar on revelation and ethics. Near semester's end an American crisis surfaced—President Nixon ordered U.S. troops into Cambodia and four students were killed by national guardsmen at Kent State. The seminar members became increasingly preoccupied with the flood of events centering on American involvement in Indochina. But the seminar materials did not speak to that in any strong, meaningful way, despite the fact that the exegesis and the moral commentary sought to deal with life-and-death issues. The main problem, the authors state, was

> the hiatus between the places where men are living and dying and being damned and brutalized, and the places that have always been the repository of resources for thinking about that.[3]

The "repository of resources" refers here to the writings available in biblical studies and Christian theology and ethics. They did not communicate a message with power and insight for this set of circumstances. Students and professors alike experienced the impotence of "theological ethics in an American crisis" (to cite the title of the case study).

There were numerous reasons for the impotence. For us it is important to note but one of them, the one that occasioned the seminar in the first place. This was the failure of communication between those working in biblical studies and those in ethics, at least communication marked by any vitality and passion around any issues worthy of common struggles. When the moral issues became intense, students and teachers both felt the failure deep inside and were not able to fill the void in the weeks that followed. It was relatively easy to see what kind of work needed to be done. It was starkly clear it had not been.

John Howard Yoder's *The Politics of Jesus* was not available

to Keck and Sellers at the time. Nor was it when Childs and
Gustafson rendered their verdicts. It might be regarded as a
welcome and glowing exception to the omission and failure indicated. It certainly is an outstanding modern work that has "a
basic orientation and grounding in the Scriptures."[4] And it is
clearly conscious of the knotty problems involved in using biblical
materials for a Christian ethic in post-biblical periods. Yoder
knows the paucity of efforts employed to bridge the gap between
biblical studies and ethics as well as the state of affairs which
necessitates a try.

> By what right does one dare seek to throw a cable
> across the chasm which usually separates the disciplines
> of New Testament exegesis and contemporary social
> ethics? Normally any link between these realms of dis-
> course would have to be extremely long and indirect.
> First there is an enormous distance between past and
> present to be covered by way of hermeneutics from exe-
> gesis to contemporary theology; then still another long
> leg must be covered from theology to ethics via secu-
> lar sociology and Ernst Troeltsch. From the perspective
> of the historical theologian, normally perched on an is-
> land between these two spans and thus an amateur on
> both banks, I can justify leaping into the problem in
> such an amateur way on only two grounds. For one
> thing, it seems that the experts who set out to go the
> long way around never get there. The Scripture scholars
> in their hermeneutic meditations develop vast systems
> of crypto-systematics, and the field of ethics remains as
> it was; or, if anything new happens there, it is usually
> fed from some other sources.
>
> The other reason for my boldness, which would be in

its own right also a subject of debate in the exegetical guild, is the radical Protestant axiom, according to which it is safer for the life of the church to have the whole people of God reading the whole body of canonical Scripture than to trust for her enlightenment only to certain of the filtering processes through which the learned men of a given age would insist all the truth must pass.[5]

It should be noted in passing that not only do "Scripture scholars in their hermeneutic meditations develop vast systems of crypto-systematics" that nonetheless leave "the field of ethics . . . as it was" but the ethicists, crowding library shelves everywhere with books and articles, have moved biblical studies not a millimeter—(this despite an occasional invitation from an occasional biblical scholar, apparently straying far from home, that ethics might in fact be an extraordinarily fruitful way into the biblical materials themselves.)[6] The chasm between these two fields is wide indeed.

Yoder's work stands, then, as the exception that makes the very point of this chapter. Few would applaud as resolutely as he any future work that would link the disciplines. But what about the relation of his treatise to this one? Our purpose is to be programmatic in a self-conscious way about the whole range of component elements in relating Christian ethics and biblical materials. His is to demonstrate the normative meaning of some crucial biblical materials for the construction of present-day Christian social ethics. Thus his highly significant volume moves on a necessarily limited number of the elements critical to relating the fields of biblical studies and Christian ethics. It is not his undertaking, as it is ours, to propose and discuss the methodological terms for making the connections. We place this volume beside his as a further contribution to spanning the chasm, a contribution on different aspects of that task. More than one cable must be thrown.

Simply to recognize the gap is not, of course, to say much about it, how it developed and the manner in which it has persisted. That needs to be done, even if in abbreviated form. One way is to trace the place of the Bible and of biblical studies in American Christian ethics and highlight those developments affecting our topic most directly.[7] Another is to note the particular development of ethics itself in an American environment. The findings unearthed will give clues for further explorations.

The American Scene. Work in ethics in the United States has developed, as James Gustafson says, "in a peculiarly American way," one in which the heaviest concentration has been given to matters of practical morality.[8] Ethicists have preferred to address particular moral issues and problems as they come to expression in the actual state of public and private behavior, rather than to address ethical issues as they emerge at more abstract philosophical and theological levels. The confrontation with issues, their analysis, the making of judgments and taking of stands, the development of strategies and solutions and the implementation of them—these have been focal emphases in American Christian ethics.

This particular concentration has had direct consequences for scholarly work. What might broadly be termed "empirical studies" have consumed more and more time and energy among ethicists. Political science and economics, the social sciences and now the life sciences and the natural sciences have emerged as major discipline areas demanding their attention. That in turn has meant the neglect of certain other areas.

. . . Americans have done little work in the history of

Christian ethics; they have done less on the relation of
ethical thought to biblical scholarship; only a few scholars have moved with ease between systematic theology
and ethics, and too little work has been done on the relation of theological ethics to philosophical ethics. American writers in Christian ethics are fundamentally interested in morals, in moral action and activity. This is not
only a Protestant mood, but also a Roman Catholic one.[9]

American ethicists, then, have been more inclined to concentrate in issue and action areas—environmental ethics, bioethics,
political ethics, economic ethics, the ethics of sexuality, ethics
and law—than they have been in discipline areas—theological
ethics, philosophical ethics, biblical ethics. Of course Christian
ethics in the United States has to some degree engaged them all.
Yet the degree of concentration and neglect has mattered considerably. What is underlined here is the relative inattention
given "the relation of ethical thought to biblical scholarship."

If this native cast explains some preoccupations that would
lead to the neglect of relating work in ethics to work in biblical
studies, it does not yet point out how the *actual* uses of the Bible
in Christian ethics also failed to bridge the gap.

A survey of these uses is instructive. It exposes both a considerable variety and a common avoidance of crucial methodological
discussions. We shall survey Protestant and Roman Catholic
works in turn.

Protestant Ethics. In its use of the Bible Protestant ethics of
the first few decades of this century reflected the dominating
(and opposing) movements in American church life, the fundamentalist and the liberal or "modernist."

The fundamentalist camp used the Bible for ethics in the

same manner as it did for theology. A biblical literalism supplied the content for both doctrine and ethics, both faith and life.
The biblical literalism meant the Bible was a book, *the* book, of
revealed morality. For ethicists of this persuasion it set forth the
normative content for Christian morality for all ages. This was
true for generalized prescription ("Thou shalt love thy neighbor
as thyself") and for highly particularized commands as well
("Thou shalt not commit adultery").

The exegetical and hermeneutical track for these ethicists was
a rather straight one. If biblical passages condemned homosexual
acts then those same acts are to be condemned by the Christian
community today and in any and all times. The underlying
assumption was that biblical ethics and Christian ethics were
synonymous. The former supplied the latter with an unchanging
and specific normative content.

On the face of it the use of the Bible among liberals appeared
to contrast markedly with that of fundamentalists. In many respects it did, perhaps most significantly in the fact that the
authority of the Bible for morality resided not in its specific
moral instruction on highly particularized matters but in its
revelation of the over-arching norms, values, and ideals binding
for the Christian life. These norms, values, and ideals supplied
the biblical content to be "applied" or "translated" by the Christian community for its moral deliberation in the present. The
need for "application" or "translation" arose from the liberals'
knowledge of the culturally conditioned character of biblical
ethics—and of those of Christians in any age.

Yet despite the significant difference here, the use of the Bible
in the writings of both camps shared an essential trait. The Bible
was a book of revealed morality that supplied the distinctive
moral content of the Christian faith. Furthermore, that content, whether expressed in propositions or in more generalized

principles and values, carried a high level of authority for the Christian life.[10]

During the 1930s and '40s a major change occurred in the use of the Bible. For many Protestant ethicists the social crises of the '20s and '30s exposed the impotence of both liberal and fundamentalist ethics. A search was undertaken for an ethic of more insight and power. That entailed a renewed attention to biblical and theological foundations. While this quest had its distinctively American cast (witness the work of Reinhold Niebuhr) the stimulus for a changing use of the Bible came from Europe. The influence was less from European biblical scholars as such, however, and more from the "crisis theology" movement that arose under Karl Barth following the shattering experience of World War I. For this movement, and for the American ethicists influenced by it, the Bible was not a book of revealed morality; it was a book of revealed reality.[11, 12]

The difference between "revealed morality" and "revealed reality" is drawn out by James Gustafson. His commentary is interpretive of H. Richard Niebuhr but it is equally valid for these ethicists as a group.

> . . . The Bible is more important for helping the Christian community to interpret the God whom it knows in its existential faith than it is for giving a revealed morality that is to be translated and applied in the contemporary world. . . . The Christian moral life, then, is not a response to moral imperatives, but to a Person, the living God.[13]
> . . . What the Bible makes known, then, is not a morality but a *reality,* a living presence to whom man responds.[14]

Barth might be cited directly to indicate a markedly different emphasis in ethics, one that employs a markedly different use of the Bible.

> . . . Ethical theory is not meant to provide man with a program the implementation of which would be his life's goal. Nor is it meant to present man with principles to be interpreted, applied, and put into practice. . . . Ethics exists to remind man of his confrontation with God, who is the light illuminating all his actions.[15]

The Bible's use by a number of ethicists, then, was as the source for discerning the organic shape of God's action in Christ. The God disclosed in the scriptures was a living, free God active in every historical present. The Christian life was centered in response to that God and that action. In current terms, the use of the Bible in ethics was more as the primary "story" for the moral life and less the source of laws, principles, ideals, and other norms. Biblical ethics *per se* were of little direct interest and importance. Biblical theology, however, was indispensable as reflection upon the all-important drama for the moral life.

The exegetical and hermeneutical endeavors of these ethicists did not aim at some rather direct move from scripture to current moral issues. Instead, the biblical work supplied the *theological* categories and framework for the deliberation of such issues as well as the materials for the nurture of Christian character.

Even in its neglect of nuance and detail this brief sketch of Protestant American ethics shows considerable diversity in the use of the Bible. For some, the scriptures provided highly specific, binding moral instruction—moral law. For others, they provided the overarching values, ideals and principles. For still others, they provided knowledge of the primary subject of ethics, God-in-Christ, and corollary knowledge of the primary relationship from which morality is to flow as the expression of faithful response.

(It might be added that these varied uses continue into the present.)

One matter in this overview requires special notice. The major change in the use of the Bible in Christian ethics was effected by the influence of European theologians, not American biblical scholars. American Protestant ethicists have not been close to biblical scholarship in the United States since early in the century. From that point on their paths have diverged.

Roman Catholic Ethics. Charles Curran refers in the following remark to the general state of affairs in Catholic writings. The work of American moral theologians is included.

> The use of the Scriptures in moral theology has varied at different historical periods, and in the period from Trent to Vatican II the role of the Scriptures in moral theology was very limited. . . . At best Scripture was employed in a proof-text fashion to corroborate arguments that were based on other reasons. . . . [16]

As in so many other respects Vatican II marks a threshold in Catholic moral theology and ethics, including their use of the Bible. Prior to that the Thomistic conceptual framework of natural/supernatural prevailed in a way it has not since. That older scheme worked itself out in a manner so as to draw noticeable distinctions between "ethics," rooted in natural law, and "moral theology," grounded in dogmatic theology. We can discuss each in turn as background to the changing use of the Bible with Vatican II.

"Ethics" in the natural law tradition rested on certain metaphysical assumptions: that reality is orderly, that it is intelligible to human reason, and that it presses upon the human will the obligation to act in accord with it. Further, that these essentials are discernible by the gift of reason common to mankind as mankind. The basic presuppositions here require nothing from the Bible in order to establish their validity; "ethics" as an enterprise can go on without any critical contributions from biblical sources. This does not mean the Bible never found a home in Catholic writings in ethics; it means any use it did find (and that *was* in fact little) corroborated what was known on other grounds. The Bible was not an essential source of the knowledge requisite for ethics.

Pre-Vatican II moral theology used scripture somewhat more frequently. This could be expected since the very notion of "moral theology" entailed the claim of a special and distinct Christian morality that went "beyond" the ethics of natural law; and this morality was rooted in a source of knowledge, revelation, that was mediated by scripture. Yet the uses of the Bible were, even here, noticeably limited in occasion and variety.[17] One reason was the strong influence of the philosophical discipline of ethics in moral theology. Much was simply taken over. And that influence was not one in which the Bible carried significant weight. Another reason was the particular kind of use the scriptures did find in moral theology. The typical course was to employ the Bible to confirm the ultimate goal of man as communion with God and to establish the existence and content of the divine law (consonant, in the Thomistic pattern, with natural law and with the eternal law in the mind of God). This vision and this law were the materials of dogma and dogmatic theology, and these in turn were the materials for moral deliberation. Thus when particular moral issues and problems were the subject at hand the turn was rarely to exegesis. Rather, casuistic reasoning was joined and specific moral admonitions were deduced as the implications of dogma and dogmatic theology. Even in moral theology, then, the use of the Bible was an indirect and limited one when it was used at all.

After World War II biblical studies across the board found a new status in Catholic education, one that continues on sure footing into the present. The rush of biblical scholarship, including work in biblical ethics,[18] was to have an impact, surfacing dramatically in Vatican II. It blurred, if not dissolved, the older distinctions between "ethics" and "moral theology." Part of this was securing for the scriptures a more pervasive and authoritative role.

Bernard Häring might be cited as one of the pathfinding moral theologians, indeed the single most influential one for American Catholics as well as Catholics worldwide. In his widely received work, *The Law of Christ,* he expounded the whole of the moral life in light of the biblically revealed norm, love, and carried on all discussion of natural law on terms set by first exegeting scripture. Lines marking off a special Christian morality from a more general human morality, and lines distinguishing moral theology from ethics, are pale in comparison with those of earlier days.[19]

What can be said about the kind of scriptural use that has come to dominate in Catholic writings? The tone and language has long since been that of values, laws, and principles. Yet even while that persisted with Vatican II a significant shift had occurred, not just in the authoritative role given biblical materials but in the way the Bible has come to be viewed for the moral life.

The shift bore a close resemblance to the changing use of the Bible in Protestant ethics that was characterized above as "revealed reality." Catholic writers, too, found themselves in the ranks of those adhering to "response" or "relational" ethics. The Bible was above all the pointer to the supreme drama in the Christian moral life, that of God's past and continuing action in Christ.

The resemblance between the Catholic and Protestant use in recent years is not coincidental. For Catholic writers, too, it was stimulated by the same scholarly streams in Europe which had felt the force of "crisis theology." While there were elements of the post-World War I renewal in Continental Protestant theology that were unacceptable to Catholics, especially the anti-philosophical and anti-natural law polemic, at precisely the point of its treatment of the Bible crisis theology was widely influential.

In summary, recent Roman Catholic writings show a significant departure from those prior to mid-century. A more central role has been given the scriptures; and a shift in the kind of use has occurred, one shared with many Protestant writers of the '50s and '60s.

Two distinctively, although not exclusively, Roman Catholic emphases remain, however. First, Catholics have given more space than Protestants (at least until very recently) to the formation of Christian character. This is wholly in keeping with the long tradition of reflection upon the "virtues." Now it is done with increased attention to biblical materials. We must mark this in passing because later we shall underscore heavily the place of character formation in the Christian moral life and the importance of the Bible for it.

The second matter is a methodological one. Roman Catholic writers, in accord with the natural law tradition, by and large adopt a generic approach to ethics. That is, Christian ethics is seen in continuity, methodologically, with the general enterprise of ethics. There is no separate and unique "Christian" methodology for Christian ethics. (Whether there is a distinctive content is a different matter.) One consequence of the generic approach involves the use and role of the Bible: what is its status as a source and authority of ethical wisdom in relation to non-biblical sources and authorities? As Curran observes,

... This generic approach will thus rely on human wisdom and reason as well as on the Scriptures, a factor that will greatly influence the role and function of the Scriptures in moral theology.[20]

Yet despite its distinctive Catholic emphases the general profile is striking in its similarity to Protestant ethics at precisely those points most central to our concerns. The conclusions drawn earlier hold equally well for the Catholic community.

1. Even while a marked change in the place and use of the Bible has occurred for many ethicists (a term inclusive of moral theologians from this point on), its origin was not in collegiality between biblical scholarship in the United States and ethicists here. Rather, it resulted from the influence of renewal in Europe, mediated through biblical theology.

2. The "peculiarly American way" in which work in ethics has developed, with its primary attention to practical moral issues and problems and its relative neglect of the relation of ethics to biblical scholarship, is, as Gustafson noted, "not only a Protestant mood, but also a Roman Catholic one." [21]

3. The attention to fundamental methodological concerns in moving between biblical materials and present-day moral matters has not been systematically undertaken any more in Roman Catholic literature than in Protestant, although a shared awareness of its importance is present.

Summary. In a word, the judgments cited above from Childs and Gustafson hold. Despite a growing interest in Christian ethics, and despite much pathfinding work in biblical studies, "there is a paucity of material that relates the two areas in a scholarly way." [22] This is the case even though there have been varied uses of the Bible and varied degrees of attention to it in Christian ethics in this century.

Biblical Studies and Ethics

Evidence for the divergence of biblical studies and Christian ethics is found on the biblical studies side in the acknowledged fact that most biblical scholars are not familiar with the categories or issues in Christian ethics. Further, in most university and seminary faculties biblical scholars are not at all in conversation with their colleagues in Christian ethics. The conversation is much livelier between biblical studies and departments of history, classics, anthropology, and literature. Christian ethicists continue to acknowledge the need for biblical resources to occupy a central place in dealing with normative ethical questions, but on the side of biblical scholarship there is little work being done and only a few expressions of any concern to relate the results of critical biblical scholarship to Christian ethics at either a methodological or a practical level.

This was not the case earlier in the century. During the fundamentalist-modernist controversy that lasted well into the thirties and divided most Protestant denominations, the nature and extent of biblical authority occupied central position. Not least among the interests on both sides of this controversy were questions about the Bible's authority for the Christian moral life. How did one relate the Bible to matters of moral behavior? Biblical scholarship was almost totally sponsored by the churches in this period, and scholars often wrote on the theological and ethical implications of their work. Christian ethics had not yet clearly emerged as a distinct discipline within the theological curriculum. Thus, a sharp line between the work of biblical studies and that of Christian ethics could not be drawn. Biblical scholars addressed ethical issues much more readily in this period than is now the case. In so doing both fundamentalist and liberal biblical scholars betrayed their peculiar theological biases in the way they saw the relation of the Bible to ethical issues.

Fundamentalist biblical scholars felt moral guidance was to be found in the Bible as a prescriptive code. Both the Old and New Testaments contained specific moral injunctions which were directly applicable to moral situations in the present. Thus, a good deal of attention was given to those portions of scripture that offered moral guidance in the form of straightforward commands and injunctions. For the Old Testament this meant treatises on the Ten Commandments and the prophets. The moralistic advice of Proverbs was also much in favor. In the New Testament, emphasis fell on the Sermon on the Mount, other teachings of Jesus on matters of ethics, and the sections of Paul's letters which addressed the ethical struggles of the early church. The assumption was that most ethical issues faced by present day Christians could be dealt with by simply finding the appropriate place in scripture where that concern is directly addressed. In ethical matters the Bible could be treated as a sort of moral code.

This fundamentalist approach to the relating of the Bible to Christian ethics was of course greatly threatened by the development of biblical criticism. If the Bible could not be taken as the literal expression of God's will in moral matters then what role could scripture have in our ethical decision-making? To admit a need for critical interpretation placed a barrier between the Bible and its direct application as a prescriptive code.

Although fundamentalism is no longer an influential position in the major Protestant denominations the prescriptive use of the Bible in Christian ethics still has strong advocates among evangelical theologians.[23] However, most of these would allow a greater area of ambiguity in translating biblical prescriptions into present-day ethical situations.

Biblical scholars were also heavily involved on the liberal side in the conflict with fundamentalism. After all the central issue was legitimacy of the critical method in biblical studies. To counter the claim of the fundamentalists that biblical criticism undermines the moral authority of the Bible, the liberals asserted that although the Bible could not be used as a code or rule book one could still find in the Bible the great moral principles that stood firm through the generations and could be used as guides to ethical decision-making by Christians of the present day. Further, the methods of critical exegesis could be a positive aid in helping to discern those principles. Great biblical ideals such as love or justice were advanced as the keys to translating biblical authority into Christian ethical behaviour. It is interesting that fundamentalist and liberal biblical scholars often found inspiration in the same locations in the Bible (e.g. the prophets and the Sermon on the Mount). The work of liberal biblical scholarship was enthusiastically taken up by theologians and church people in the Social Gospel movement. They found in the themes of the prophets and in Jesus' preaching of the kingdom of God great biblical themes which could be placed at the center of their efforts to raise the social consciousness of the church.

There were those among the liberal biblical scholars, however, who saw the task of biblical studies solely in terms of critical, objective scholarship. They saw their task as the thorough understanding of the Bible in its historical context; it remained for others to relate it to theology or ethics.[24] By the thirties it was clear that the liberals had won the battle with fundamentalism, and biblical studies became increasingly characterized by scholarship which exhibited little interest in biblical theology (at least in any normative sense) and of course, very little concern for relating the Bible to ethical behaviour. Men such as William A. Irwin, Robert Pfeiffer, and Henry Cadbury were among the chief opponents of a later revival of interest in biblical theology in the forties.

Although both fundamentalist and liberal biblical scholars exhibited an interest in relating the Bible to Christian ethics their approaches were severely limited. Both of these groups did violence to the integrity of the biblical canon by selecting what suited their perspective. Many portions of the scripture received little or no attention. The rich pluralism of biblical perspectives was usually ignored in relating to ethical issues. In addition, neither group gave adequate attention to the particulars of how one moves from the biblical rules or principles to the present moral situation. Both fundamentalists and liberals displayed a simplistic naivete concerning the dynamics of this transition. This left neither camp in a position to cope creatively with the complex ethical issues of the mid-twentieth century.

Following World War II and into the late fifties American biblical scholarship became dominated by a "biblical theology movement." [25] Although influenced by European theologians such as Barth and Brunner the movement was peculiarly American because of its setting against the background of the fundamentalist-liberal battles of the twenties and thirties. A renewed emphasis on biblical theology seemed to offer a third alternative, "the possibility of accepting biblical criticism without reservation as a valid tool while at the same time recovering a robust, confessionally oriented theology." [26] An entire generation of younger biblical scholars came to the forefront in this movement. Men such as G. Ernest Wright, Bernhard Anderson, and James Muilenburg in Old Testament and Paul Minear, Floyd Filson, and Otto Piper in New Testament were among its leading lights.

The biblical theology movement was characterized by a number of major concerns. Chief among these was a call to rediscover the theological message of the Bible and to move beyond biblical criticism as an end in itself. There was a great interest to make the Bible's message available for appropriation in the life of the church. The movement's other emphases included a stress on the unity of the Old and New Testaments, an espousal of history as the primary category for understanding God's revealing of himself to the biblical communities, the claim for a unique biblical mentality (Hebrew as contrasted to Greek), and an argument for the distinctiveness of biblical faith when compared with the other cultures of the ancient world. All of these emphases contributed to the conviction held by scholars that they were reaffirming the relevance of the Bible for a modern age. This showed clearly in the great interest within the movement in exegesis, preaching, and theological education.

With these interests one would think that the scholars of the biblical theology movement would have exhibited a great concern for relating biblical studies to Christian ethics, but such was not the case. With the exception of Amos Wilder,[27] who was not a part of the biblical theology movement, one looks in vain for significant American works published in the forties and fifties relating the Bible to ethical concerns. The few important works in this period were from England or Europe.[28]

The main interest for this new biblical theology in relating to the contemporary world was in the renewal of the life of the church, which was seen as the chief locus of God's activity. The focus was on ecclesiology rather than ethics. Because of this biblical theology played a prime role in the growth of the ecumenical movement during this period. The lack of interest in ethical issues was to be partly the undoing of the biblical theology movement.

In the late fifties and early sixties ethical issues came to the forefront of the church's agenda. Church people were less interested in the renewal of the institutional church than in the church's role in the renewal of society. The new biblical theology was ill-equipped to assist the church in meeting this challenge. Its emphasis on a God who acts in history seemed to identify his present action with an institutional church in which many had lost confidence. At the very least many saw God at work in secular movements with equal power. Its call to rediscover the biblical mentality and the uniqueness of biblical religion seemed to many to represent an archaizing tendency. New and relevant exegetical works, and newly empowered preaching failed to materialize. Brevard Childs notes:

> It remained a disturbing fact that the traditionally strong and aggressive interest of Americans in social ethics continued to thrive, and indeed attract the most promising of the theological students, without being seriously influenced from the side of biblical studies. . . . When the Bible was used in ethical discussions, it was a question whether it was those elements close to the heart of the Biblical Theology Movement which attracted attention.[29]

By the early sixties what had looked like a growing consensus for a new biblical theology a decade earlier had ceased to be a major force either in biblical studies or in the wider theological community. The demise of this biblical theology movement left those working in Christian ethics with the "growing suspicion that an integral relation between biblical studies and the theory and practice of social ethics was extremely nebulous."[30] The result was a wider gap than ever between these two disciplines.

Biblical scholarship in the sixties and seventies has moved sharply away from any significant concern for relating to the constructive task of the theologian or the ethicist. The turning point was marked by the important article on biblical theology by

Krister Stendahl in the *Interpreter's Dictionary of the Bible*.[31]
He argued that the legitimate task of biblical theology was descriptive. The biblical scholar is primarily a historian dealing
with the gathering of objectively verifiable data from the ancient
sources. As such, his task is to be separated sharply from that of
the theologian (or one might add, ethicist) which was constructive. The biblical scholar simply hands over his data to those
who wish to wrestle with its normative authority for the community of faith.

Stendahl's position was the direct antithesis of the biblical
theology movement, but it met with a ready response. Current
biblical scholarship is largely dominated by this view of the biblical scholar as scientific, objective historian. One of the primary
reasons for this development is the movement of the center of
biblical studies from the seminary to the university. The growth
of college and university departments of religion in the sixties
resulted in a greater interest within the scholarly guild for conversation with the other disciplines of the university curriculum
than with the other disciplines of the theological curriculum, including Christian ethics. Much of biblical scholarship is currently
divorced from the life of the church or its concerns. This is not
of course illegitimate. Our knowledge and understanding of biblical history, language, literature, and backgrounds have been
greatly advanced by this work. But this development has left
the concerns of those who view the Bible as scripture and as
somehow authoritative for the life of the church poorly tended.
The ancient communities originally preserved the biblical traditions with the intention of evoking a faith response anew in succeeding generations. There must also be those biblical scholars
who are concerned with that dimension of the biblical material.
Perhaps the church itself should share much of the responsibility

for the current situation in that it has done little in recent times to sponsor or encourage basic biblical research in its behalf.

Under the influence of these developments most of the recent works on biblical ethics have been descriptive. They describe the ethical perspectives and struggles of the ancient biblical communities. For the Old Testament this may be represented by James Muilenburg's *The Way of Israel: Biblical Faith and Ethics*,[32] and by the inclusion of J. Hempel's article on "Ethics in the Old Testament" in the *Interpreter's Dictionary of the Bible*.[33] In the New Testament this type of work is represented by two recently published works, *Ethics and the New Testament* by J. L. Houlden[34] and *Ethics in the New Testament* by Jack T. Sanders.[35] The helpful book by Victor Furnish, *Theology and Ethics in Paul* should also be listed here.[36]

There have been some attempts on the part of biblical scholars, particularly in New Testament, to open up some conversation with contemporary Christian ethics. Works by John Knox,[37] William Baird,[38] Victor Furnish,[39] and Walter Brueggeman[40] have suggested relationships between their biblical findings and present-day ethical issues. Also helpful have been several joint efforts of biblical scholars and Christian ethicists.[41] However, none of these works addresses the methodological questions of the relationship between biblical studies and Christian ethics. How is scripture appropriated for the formation of character and conduct in the Christian community? Among biblical scholars this question is mainly greeted with silence. Brevard Childs addresses a helpful chapter to this question in a larger work.[42] H. Edward Everding and Dana W. Wilbanks (a New Testament scholar and a Christian ethicist) have dealt with the Bible's role in ethical decisions in a new book.[43] But for the most part we can only conclude that the divergence of biblical studies from Christian ethics remains a reality in the guild of biblical scholarship.

The Bible and Ethical Concerns in the Church

We have been speaking of a growing divergence between biblical studies and Christian ethics as academic disciplines within the theological curriculum. Needless to say this divergence has also contributed to a growing gap between biblical resources and ethical concerns in the life of the church. Most denominational bodies and a large number of local congregations have experienced some form of split between traditionalists, who claim to value the Bible but avoid issue involvement, and social activists, who are deeply involved with ethical issues but disdain the resources of the church's biblical and theological heritage. This division in one form or another has sometimes emerged in open conflict, and at other times remained simply as differences of emphasis within congregations and judicatories. Nevertheless, it is true that within the local church little genuine interaction of scriptural resources with ethical concerns has taken place. Those concerned with the ethical dilemmas facing the church have regarded the Bible as either irrelevant or so indirectly related to issues as to make its use too time consuming in the face of urgent ethical issues. A concerned pastor remarked, "If people are starving there is no time to be reading the Bible." Those who do read and study the Bible in the churches have often done so for reasons of personal piety, and their labors seldom bear fruit in terms of informing the church's missional involvement in the difficult questions of our day.

Jurgen Moltmann has noticed this same division with the church today and has called it an "identity-involvement dilemma." [44] If the church becomes too preoccupied with its own identity it becomes an enclave removed from the struggles of the human community. It "becomes a fossil church . . . an unimportant sect on the edge of rapidly changing and progressive society." On the other hand, when the church seeks to involve itself in the social and political struggles of our time there is a tendency to become swallowed up by secular movements and to lose touch with any particular identity as the church. The study of the social sciences seems more relevant than scripture or theology. Moltmann warns of becoming a "religion of society" (albeit a progressive one) and calls this a "chameleon theology" adapting its colors to blend with the surroundings. "But, Christian theology should not adapt itself in order to hide; it is required rather to reveal what is specifically its own in the changing times." It is the separation of identity and involvement within the church that has rendered the church powerless in a time of crisis.

It is ironic that the gap between scriptural resources and moral concerns has grown so great during a time when ethical issues have risen to the top of the agenda in most churches. Earlier in the century much of the church's energy was directed toward the clarification of theological issues. With the development of the ecumenical movement many church bodies struggled with the questions on the nature of the church and the path to its unity. But in the sixties and seventies it was ethical issues that came to the forefront in the churches' attempts to respond to the demand for racial justice and to speak to the division within the nation brought by the war in Indochina. Ethical issues still stand most prominently in the list of matters seeking the churches' attention. What is the church's role in the clarification of national values for post-Watergate America? How do we respond to the tragedy of global hunger and poverty in ways which recognize the contribution our affluence has made to this suffering? How do Christians decide responsibly about abortion, homosexuality, changing roles of men and women, environmental stewardship, racial bigotry?

Such a preponderance of ethical issues facing the modern church makes it especially important to reestablish significant contact with biblical foundations. This importance of the Bible may not be clear when we consider the majority of ordinary ethical decisions Christians make. Many values and choices are already clear in the Christian community. They have been internalized already and may be reinforced by societal practice as well. For example, Christians may not need to consult the Bible to make moral decisions about the stealing of another person's possessions. Many ethical decisions are made out of established values nurtured in the Christian community. To be sure these questions may arise in morally ambiguous situations that need clarification, or strategies may need to be developed for embodying moral values in social policy but this still may not call for any basic reexamination of biblical foundations.

It is when the church wrestles with issues for which the moral guidelines do not seem clear that it becomes fundamentally important to do so in relation to the scriptural inheritance of the faith. The need for such basic ethical struggle in the church arises in several ways. 1) The church may meet new situations that have not previously been encountered. This would certainly be the case in connection with the moral dilemmas posed by new capabilities for genetic alteration or organ transplants. 2) New understandings may challenge commonly held positions in church or society. Current debate on homosexuality as an acceptable Christian lifestyle has been fueled by the assertion that new insight into the nature of human sexuality calls for a reexamination of the church's traditional position. 3) The church may find itself in conflict with prevailing cultural norms. During the war in Indochina many Christians found themselves in opposition to national policy. This touched off a far reaching ethical debate on issues of war and peace, national responsibility and individual conscience. In situations such as these when the pastor or lay-person finds himself in a situation where clear understandings are not available within the church, he must know how to go to the basic biblical and theological resources and relate the particular identity of the Christian community to the demands of the present moral situation.

If the Bible is indeed to play a role in these moral struggles some current tendencies in the modern church must be countered.

1. Large segments of the church in the United States have lost touch with the Bible. As a result much of the church's attempt to deal with ethical issues suffers from a kind of identity-less drift. Numerous voices have noted the complete lack of knowledge about the content and meaning of the scriptures among many modern church people.[45] The Bible can be almost totally absent as a factor in the life of a significant number of congregations. This creates a confused focus for the church's witness to ethical issues because it does not address issues as a community with any biblical and historical particularity. There is nothing to distinguish the church from many other concerned groups in our society when it speaks to moral concerns. At worst this can contribute to an impression of relativism in the church's witness. Any position can be labeled Christian if it does not have to be held accountable to biblical and theological understandings of what it means to be the church. More often the church's stand on issues seems to arise out of a vague humanism that seldom taps the biblical material for insight. A recent issue of a denominational journal on social concerns devoted an entire issue to global hunger. The opening editorial urged hunger as a priority concern for local churches and a later article suggested that churches could become bases for re-educating the American public away from the values of affluence. Nothing else in the issue

betrayed a hint that the church was speaking or being addressed. The literature of denominational boards dealing with ethical concerns often shows the same tendency. It speaks with the voice of the social analyst and not the church struggling to relate its particular identity to the moral questions present in our day. The Bible is the basis of that identity, and if the church is to participate in the moral renewal of the society it must discover the resources there.

2. In ethical matters the church is also plagued by individualism. When pressed on a given issue the appeal is usually to one's own individual impressions and reactions. The war in Viet Nam and Watergate along with other events of recent years have caused many to lose confidence in the authority of institutions. The result seems to be a resurgence of individualism in society. This is readily apparent in the church where many are unwilling to subscribe to any authority beyond the self, particularly in wrestling with sensitive moral issues. Congregations may discuss issues, but the notion of biblical or theological tradition as authoritative in any sense is carefully absent, and it is often left to the individual to draw conclusions about or to decide on a response to a given issue. A young African pastor, prominent in the struggle for justice and freedom in Rhodesia, actively participated along with his family in the life of a United Methodist congregation in Washington, D.C., for two years while he was doing additional study. When he returned to Rhodesia he was arrested without charges being brought, and there was fear for his ultimate safety. The pastor of the church assumed that the congregation would want to be among the first to voice its protest in appropriate channels to this imprisonment of a man they knew to represent moderate and principled Christian leadership much needed in his community. To the pastor's astonishment no

body of the church would take any official action. They felt action should be left to individuals since not all members might want to participate in what would be a political protest. Of course, in the absence of courageous action by the congregational leadership few individuals took action either. There is a great suspicion of corporate responsibility and identity in the church largely because that would require the acknowledgement of God's Word as an authority transcending individual autonomy to create a community of witness that is more than a collection of selves.

Biblical scholarship has greatly advanced our ability to understand the meaning of the biblical message in the context of its own time. Christian ethics has similarly advanced our understanding of the factors and process involved in the formation of moral identity and in moral decision-making in any present-day context. These understandings are available to the church (although one could wish in more usable form), and they will be drawn upon in this study. What the church needs, and does not yet seem to have available to it, is a clearer methodology for bridging the gap to relate the biblical word to character formation and decision-making in the modern church.

The goal of this book is to address that problem of relationship and to begin the development of a clearer methodology. Among the issues of importance with which we intend to deal are the following.

1. What controls our use of scripture? What can prevent us from choosing passages merely to support an already fixed position? How do we judge between conflicting positions both claiming biblical support?

2. What is the nature of the Bible's authority in moral matters? Is it absolute or conditioned by time and circumstances? Are all of the parts equally authoritative? What kind of authority

can the Bible have in dealing with ethical issues not known in ancient times, e.g. overpopulation?

3. How are biblical resources related to other sources of insight? In addressing the dimensions of the Christian moral life the church will surely want to employ many valuable perspectives from secular sources. The wealth of material available from the social sciences and the natural sciences is especially important. Does this material supplement the biblical? Can it supercede the scriptural material? What is the authority of such non-biblical resources?

4. Where does the use of the Bible fit in the development of moral character or in decision-making and action? Should it always be the beginning point? Can it be brought in at different points? Would it then play different roles?

5. How does the corporate context of the church affect our use of the Bible for ethics? Is corporate accountability necessary? How does the church prepare for its role?

If some new perspective can be brought to these questions perhaps some small contribution will be made toward changing the pattern of divergence to one of reunion.

2 relating the bible and christian ethics: recent efforts

There is an important two-part consensus held by biblical scholars and Christian ethicists alike. The first can be stated most succinctly by saying that Christian ethics is not synonymous with biblical ethics. Again and again the demonstration in biblical studies has been that of the cultural and historical "conditioned-ness" of the scriptures, sufficiently so that biblical morality cannot, without violation of its own integrity, leap over the centuries to be applied in some unqualified way to different historical circumstances and different modes of life and thought. Such a procedure would fail to take seriously history and the God of history—a course the scriptures of Judaism and Christianity reject with almost unparalleled vigor among the world religions.

From the side of Christian ethics, and not only biblical studies, there are reasons to reject an equating of biblical ethics and Christian ethics. One obvious reason is that the biblical communities did not confront some of the factors and ethical issues that shape to an extraordinary degree the moral matrix of our lives—a world population doubling every three-and-one-half decades, a planet whose environmental carrying capacity is being taxed in ways it has never been, a technology that is altering societies in ways that surpass the boundaries of even recent imagination, a science that has tossed whole areas of concern, such as bio-ethics, into a forest of moral question marks and exclamation points. The list could be extended by reading almost any daily newspaper or walking around almost any parish. If there is "a word from the Lord" on these moral matters unknown to the biblical communities—and we trust there is—it is not one simply ferreted from biblical morality and then somehow "applied" in and for our time.

Another reason is the conditionedness mentioned above. Christian ethics today would not find sound justification even for accepted biblical codes regarding slavery, treatment of women, or the set of crimes exacting capital punishment, to cite but a few examples. "Time" has made some "ancient good uncouth."

In short, biblical ethics is not and cannot be the same as Christian ethics for us. It is in fact precisely *because* they are not that the questions of interpretation and relationship arise which this volume seeks to address.

The other part of the consensus is that for Christian ethics the Bible is somehow normative. *In what way normative* is a question with many proposed answers; but there is agreement that the Bible *is* the charter document that holds a place more authoritative than any other source. This would be the case if on no other count than that the Bible is the only major source of knowledge about the ultimate object of Christian allegiance in the moral life, God in Jesus Christ. Or, if on no other count than that the Bible is the major source of the whole primal story at the center of the church's and the Christian's identity. The list of reasons for this high authority could be extended—and will be later. Suffice it to note for the moment this second matter of agreement:

Christian ethics is not Christian ethics unless the Bible is normative in some important way for the Christian life.

If biblical scholars and Christian ethicists are then agreed on
these two matters the important question becomes how the Bible
and ethics in the contemporary community of faith are to be
related, both in theory and in practice. It is precisely this methodological question which is least often taken up in the literature, and which this book hopes to address.

The first step in that constructive task is to examine those
voices that have spoken directly to the methodological question
of relating scripture and Christian ethics. We stress "directly"
because we cannot provide assessment of those many biblical
scholars who have ventured commentary in moral matters, or
that majority of Christian ethicists who have drawn upon biblical materials and biblical scholarship in ways central to their
ethical concerns. Such a study would be one of importance, deserving of a separate volume. In the meantime, what we can do
is note in some detail selected recent efforts by both biblical
scholars and Christian ethicists to discuss directly the relationship
of the Bible and ethics. We do this in order to suggest the extent
of our indebtedness to important previous work on which we are
building, but also to indicate areas not yet clarified or issues not
yet addressed.

James M. Gustafson

Among Christian ethicists James M. Gustafson is noted for his
concern to carefully ground moral judgment in the biblical and
historical tradition. This shows clearly in a work such as *Christ
and the Moral Life*.[1] He is also one of only a handful of ethicists
to directly address the methodological question, how does scripture actually function in relation to Christian ethics. His article

"The Place of Scripture in Christian Ethics: A Methodological Study"[2] is widely regarded as of central importance. A consideration of Gustafson's contribution in this article seems a fitting beginning point for the discussion of this chapter.

Gustafson sets out as his intention a discussion of how scripture relates to moral judgments about actions. He rules out broader questions on scripture's role in determining the morality of alternative courses of action or what means and ends are employed. Since the article was written in 1970 he uses as a concrete case the question of the morality of the American invasion of Cambodia in that year.

Of particular importance is Gustafson's typology of the ways scripture is used in making moral judgments. The first is its use as moral law. "Those actions of persons and groups which violate the moral law revealed in Scripture are to be judged morally wrong."[3] Gustafson points out the great difficulty of determining the content of the moral law in scripture and further the complex decisions about how it is to be applied in judging a particular issue.

A second use of scripture is to judge actions according to their success at embodying the moral ideals set forth in the Bible. Here again this use must reckon with the difficulties of determining both the content and application of a moral idea from scripture. There is room for great variety of judgment here. Both of these first two uses have been touched on in Chapter One since they largely correspond to the two poles of the fundamentalist-liberal controversy earlier in the century. It is Gustafson's third and fourth uses which suggest options we have not yet noted.

The third use is one of analogy. "Those actions of persons and groups are to be judged morally wrong which are similar to actions that are judged to be wrong or against God's will under similar circumstances in Scripture, or are discordant with actions judged to be right or in accord with God's will in Scripture."[4] The great difficulty, of course, is determining what constitutes a genuine analogy. Gustafson properly identifies the issue as one of control. If present events control then the danger is one of searching for biblical support for a judgment already made on other grounds. If scripture is in control one is faced with deciding which themes are really normative for biblical morality and can therefore be used as analogies.

This issue of control is also important for the fourth use of scripture. Gustafson describes this fourth use as "looser than the first three."

> Scripture witnesses to a great variety of moral values, moral norms and principles through many different kinds of biblical literature: moral law, visions of the future, historical events, moral precepts, paraenetic instruction, parables, dialogues, wisdom sayings, allegories. They are not in a simple way reducible to a single theme; rather they are directed to particular historical contexts. The Christian community judges the actions of persons and groups to be morally wrong, or at least deficient, on the basis of reflective discourse about present events *in the light of* appeals to this variety of material as well as to other principles and experiences. Scripture is one of the informing sources for moral judgments, but it is not sufficient in itself to make any particular judgment authoritative.[5]

Such a use of scripture becomes a process with many factors to be weighed. In such a "loose" use the question of control becomes especially important. What keeps our use of the Bible from being totally relativized by individual and cultural factors? A number of emphases in Gustafson's discussion are helpful in answering this question.

1. More than most who have addressed the issue Gustafson recognizes the tremendous diversity within the scriptures. Any single narrow usage of the Bible could not properly utilize the variety of resources there. Moral law, for example, would select only the prescriptive statements of the Bible, such as the Decalogue, neglecting the important moral resources in parables, historical events, and wisdom sayings. Gustafson does not make it explicit, but he seems to imply that within his looser use of scripture there are a variety of ways biblical resources might be employed, and these might well include elements of moral law, moral ideal, and moral analogy.

2. Gustafson stresses that scripture alone is not a sufficient basis for making moral judgments. Scripture must always be in dialog with nonscriptural sources. On the one hand this includes the "continuing tradition of Christian morality beyond the closing of the canon." [6] He might also have added the continuing tradition of biblical interpretation. This on-going tradition within the Christian community is not just a pedantic drawing of implications from the biblical materials. It is a witness to belief in a God who not only acted historically in biblical events but is actively present in the events of each new age. Moral judgments cannot rest on scripture alone because this is not the only place where the church can discern God's activity. The Bible may assist us in seeing what God is doing and requiring of us in the present, but in order to fully see we must also draw upon resources outside the Christian community. Gustafson reminds us that we share many principles and values with those outside the Christian community, and in making moral judgments we ought properly

to be in dialog with secular disciplines such as the social and natural sciences as well as with scripture and theology.

3. Throughout his article, Gustafson implies the importance of the church as a context for this dialogic use of scripture. Although he constantly refers to the Christian community he does not explicitly develop a statement on its role. Elsewhere Gustafson has placed great stress on the importance of the church as a "community of moral discourse." [7] One assumes that it is within the church that a dialogic use of scripture in making moral judgments is possible. How the church prepares for and executes that role is a question we shall take up at a later point.

4. Gustafson is especially helpful in showing that scripture is not limited to any single point of input in the process of making moral judgments. Using his example of the Cambodian invasion, he demonstrates that scripture informs the "meaning of the history in which the events take place, the motives and intentions of the decision-makers, the circumstances in which it is deemed proper to act, and the consequences of the action." [8] This implies that the precise range of biblical materials used and the modes of their applicability must vary depending on what point in the process of moral assessment one wishes to address. The implications of this reach far beyond the scope of Gustafson's treatment.

At least two questions are left open in Gustafson's treatment and must be mentioned as matters requiring further attention in a later chapter.

1. The first is the matter of biblical authority. If the scripture is to be used in a dialogic fashion with non-scriptural sources both from within and from outside the Christian tradition, then how does its authority differ from those other sources? Gustafson recognizes this as a crucial question left indefinite in his sug-

gested "looser use" of scripture. His own understanding of the nature of biblical authority is suggested by his statement that the Bible's "understanding of God and his purposes, of man's condition and needs, of precepts, events, human relationships, however, do provide the basic *orientation* toward particular judgments." [9] We are still left with the basic question of what weight the authority of scripture as "basic orientation" is to be given in making a moral judgment. Gustafson suggests that the character of biblical authority in moral judgments is largely dependent on theological and philosophical decisions about one's understanding of God's revealing of himself and one's understanding of the task of ethics. These questions of authority focused by Gustafson must be addressed at a later point.

2. A second question is that of implications for biblical exegesis. Gustafson really never gives attention to this since he speaks as a Christian ethicist within the framework of that discipline. But his insight into the place of scripture in Christian ethics clearly raises questions for the biblical scholar as well as the ethicist. What is the role of critical exegetical method in making the scripture available to the community in its moral judgments? Surely exegetical methodology needs to be taken as seriously as ethical analysis. One suspects it is in need of the same clarification that Gustafson gives us on the dynamics of moral judgment. Elsewhere Gustafson has observed that "few biblical scholars have provided studies upon which writers in ethics can draw." [10]

Still to be answered is the question of what the criteria for usable exegetical studies would be, not only for scholars in Christian ethics but for the church seeking to relate the scriptures to responsible ethical life. The scope and character of exegesis done for and within the church has not yet been fully discussed in the literature on the relationship of the Bible and Christian ethics. One suspects that a clearer determination at this point would provide a significant element of control in Gustafson's own looser use of scripture. Sound exegesis would become the prerequisite to any significant dialog between scripture and other sources of moral insight. Although this area lay beyond the scope of Gustafson's treatment it cannot be ignored in any larger discussion of scripture and ethics.

Since the article we have been discussing confines itself to scripture's role in moral judgments about actions there are certain areas of Gustafson's concerns as an ethicist which do not see full light there. One of these is his attention in many writings to the formation of persons as moral agents. In a paper presented to the Pittsburgh Festival on the Gospels entitled "The Relation of the Gospels to the Moral Life" Gustafson suggests that we think about the role the Gospels play in the formation of the moral agent.

> The Gospels can be related to the moral life . . . by interpreting them to influence the development of the "sort of persons" members of the community become. Here I wish to accent not the impact that moral precepts have on the determination of particular acts, but the impact that the Gospels have on the formation of the agent, the person, who acts. The question to be explored is "In what ways do, can and should the Gospels qualify or accent the persisting characteristics of the person as moral agent? In what ways do they affect his attitudes, his dispositions, his basic orientation of intentionality toward the world and other persons?" [11]

He then continues on to develop the thesis that the "Gospels provide paradigms of action, intention, and disposition which flow into and inform the manner of life, the bearing toward one another that arises from and is worthy of the gospel." [12]

Gustafson's thesis could be broadened to speak about the role of the scripture as a whole. Most attempts to relate the Bible to Christian ethics have focused solely on decision-making, the application of biblical resources to particular issues. Almost no attention has been paid to the role of the Bible in the basic formation of Christian character. We will want to return to this unexplored area.

Gustafson's work has pointedly reminded us that there is more than one way in which scripture is related to morality. A comprehensive view of the relationship between the Bible and Christian ethics must take them all into account.

Edward LeRoy Long Jr.

Edward LeRoy Long Jr. poses the general issue at the very outset of his article, "The Use of the Bible in Christian Ethics."

> Christians generally understand Scripture to be a guide for both faith and practice. Even the most casual observer knows, however, that Christians interpret the meaning of Scripture for matters of faith in quite different ways. The hermeneutic problems that arise in interpreting the Bible as an authority for faith do not evaporate when the Bible is consulted with regard to moral practice. . . . [13]

Long does not, however, systematically discuss the hermeneutical problems in order to offer a constructive proposal for relating Bible and ethics. Rather, he describes the different ways in which the Bible has functioned as a source for Christian ethics. They so closely parallel those discussed earlier that we need only mention them here. For some, "moral guidance can be had from the

Bible in prescriptive terms;"[14] for others, the Bible is the source of the guiding ethical ideals and principles for the Christian life;[15] for still others, the Bible shows a pattern of response for the moral life, rooted in an organic relationship of trust in and worship of God in Christ.[16]

This typology has been a useful one, written early (1965) and drawn upon by most of the scholars pursuing the relating of biblical studies and Christian ethics. Beyond acknowledging its importance for this reason, we want to take note of two additional items.

1. Long cannot dismiss any of these three ways as unbiblical. He finds compelling representatives among biblical scholars and among theologians and ethicists for each use. All marshall much evidence to make their cases. This does not mean there are not stronger and weaker cases, or that there are not proper and improper uses of scripture. Nor does it mean the task of critical assessment has been set aside. It means that any judgment about the relative adequacy of each use must be a judgment made about the work of thoughtful and sophisticated scholars who have already anticipated and replied to some of the possible objections to their positions.

Judgments about the relative adequacy of the uses of scripture is made the more complex, Long finds, by virtue of the fact there is little agreement among the biblical scholars themselves. That is, the professional students of the Bible disagree about the function of the tradition and scriptures *in the biblical communities* as they deliberated moral questions. Thus the guild of biblical scholars cannot supply consensus about the "biblical" use of scriptures in moral matters. Much less is there anything approaching consensus about the proper function of the Bible for *present* moral deliberation.

The discovered pluralism in both the biblical communities and in the church today, and the lack of even rough consensus is apparently the reason Long fails to declare himself for one or another of the options outlined. It is apparently also the reason he does not offer a methodology for relating Bible and ethics. Recent scholarship has in his judgment raised far more questions than it has answered about the function and authority of scripture for ethics.

Long's own caution entails a caution for us. The wrong procedure would be to assume *one right way* of using scripture in Christian ethics. Foreclosing on the options outlined by choosing only one or the other would lead to an unnecessarily constricted methodology. Long's later work in ethics, though not directed to our subject specifically, would seem correct in its call for "comprehensive complementarity." [17] A sophisticated methodology would be able to say when and on what terms multiple uses of scripture might be employed in ethics. In any case, there is no reason to ensconce ourselves at the outset in the well-lit den of a singular use of scripture. Indeed, that may well be the most unbiblical way of all.

2. The interplay of theological and ethical frames of reference and the use of the Bible is an intriguing one in the material supplied by Long. What is clear—and important—is that there is no one-to-one relationship between the particular use of the Bible and the user's theological and moral assumptions. Representatives of the prescriptive use of scripture vary enormously with respect to their theological positions and moral commitments. The same generalization holds with equal force for representatives of the other two motifs in Long's typology.

It would be false to conclude that no meaningful connection exists between the use of scripture and the theological and moral commitments held. Rather, the relationship is sufficiently complex to allow multiple variations.

The implication for our task would seem to be that while any proposed methodology for the relating of biblical materials to current moral concerns will of necessity entail its own theological and ethical assumptions, a methodology might nonetheless be constructed that can be shared widely, across boundaries that otherwise separate theological systems and ethical theories. The methodology proposed in later chapters will claim this broad range of compatibility, one that crosses diverse outlooks in theology and ethics.

Charles Curran

Charles Curran also discusses the relationship of theological stances, ethical commitments and the uses of scripture.[18] His remarks amplify and enrich the discussion initiated by Long.

In the practice of appropriating biblical materials, which are themselves highly diverse in their understanding of the moral life, the actual use or uses will of necessity be selective. This selection will be made in accord with the theological and ethical presuppositions of the user. Thus the assumptions and commitments *brought to* the Bible play *a*, if not *the*, key interpretive role.

The inevitable selection can work itself out in one or more ways, however.

1. Theological and ethical commitments often mandate a selection of scriptural content that in fact serves as an interpretation of the scriptures as a whole. The selection serves as the interpretive key for the entire corpus. What is regarded as the central message gives coherence to the diverse materials. It is the "authoritative" scripture, the canon within the canon, that signals "what

in the end it is all about." The theological and ethical commitments work upon the texts in such a way as to secure this kind of unity for the whole. In this case, then, the particular use of scripture as a source of ethical wisdom, and the view of the scriptures as a whole, is best understood in light of the prior theological and moral commitments. The reader's theology and ethics "order" the scripture.

2. Biblical materials, even those *already* selected, have their own power, however, and often shape the theological and ethical perspectives of the reader and hearer. In fact, they may, as they often have, work in such a way as to set and shape the agenda for theology and ethics. That is, those concerns most in keeping with the biblical motifs and accorded authority are placed within the field of vision and concern for theology and ethics. Those not in keeping are neglected and fall outside the pale. The biblical materials thus may help establish the boundaries of the Christian's outlook and put his or her theology and ethics in order.

There is, then, a circularity involved in the interplay of theological and moral commitments and the appropriation of biblical materials, a hermeneutical or interpretive circle. Prior notions of what counts as theological and ethical assumptions and convictions work an inescapable selectivity among biblical sources. Yet the biblical materials can and often do fashion the basic perspectives of theology and ethics.

If selectivity in the use of the Bible for ethics is unavoidable—and it is—then it is a *necessary* risk. That risk entails at least two dangers.

1. The biblical materials chosen can, if no methodological safeguards are provided, unnecessarily limit the range of vision and the agenda deemed proper for Christian ethics.

2. The biblical materials chosen can, if no methodological safeguards are provided, unnecessarily restrict the biblical sources themselves that might bear upon the moral life.[19]

The significance of this unavoidable selectivity is a double one for methodology. One major methodological task is that of bringing to expression the operating theological assumptions and moral commitments of individuals. Only then can their role in interpretation and appropriation of the biblical sources be seen and assessed. A second task, one of equal importance, is tracing out the consequences of selection, not only for the moral matter at hand but for the very notion of what counts and what doesn't count for Christian ethics. Then the connection can be noted between the use of the Bible as a source for ethics and the determination of moral vision itself. These tasks require a community of regular reflection and accountability in the relating of the Bible and ethics, a matter we shall address in Chapter Four.

Another intriguing item in Curran's discussion, one vital to our discussion in the next chapter, is his conjecture that the Bible carries different weight and influence for different elements in the moral life of the Christian. He first outlines these elements, then speculates about the relation of scripture to them.

The first consists of the basic "stance, horizon or posture" of the Christian.[20] By this Curran means the whole bearing of the Christian, the way in which he or she sees and understands reality. In Curran's view, this element is the single most important one for the moral life. It is fundamentally expressive of who we are and what we're about.

The second element is what Curran calls "the general model for understanding the Christian moral life." [21] We can pose the matter in question form: What portrayal or description of the Christian life best depicts the life of God with man in its implications for human conduct? Curran himself finds the model of relationality and responsibility most "faithful," although he realizes this is but one among several possibilities. In any case, the chosen portrayal of the Christian life will be a crucial component of the person's ethics.

There are other elements, each of separate influence and importance. Curran simply lists them: 1) the values, goals, or ideals of the Christian; 2) the Christian's dispositions or attitudes, or virtues; 3) the norms chosen by the Christian to measure conduct and make decisions; 4) the process or procedures used in making judgments and decisions.

Even without further discussion, these elements are sufficiently clear and distinct that the reader can follow Curran's assignment of the place and influence of scripture for each of them. His suggestion is a sliding scale of applicability and importance. For the two most "general"—and most important—elements (the basic bearing of the Christian and the model for understanding the moral life) the Bible is a decisive shaping force. Its influence and authority are greatest here. As one moves through the other elements ("the ... more specific ethical considerations"[22] listed in the preceding paragraph) the biblical materials wield less influence and share a more even authority with non-biblical sources.

All this can be expressed differently. The Bible's most decisive appropriation for ethics is at the point of forging the Christian's self-understanding and in presenting and portraying the normative pattern of the Christian moral life. Its significance and its distinctive use for ethics diminishes in those areas of moral content and moral deliberation more generally shared among Christians and non-Christians alike.

Two matters should be highlighted here for later consideration.

1. Any methodology for the use of the Bible in ethics should be "as comprehensive as possible by considering all the elements

that go into ethical consideration." [23] That is, the role and author- ity of scripture should be designated for matters ranging from the Christian's self-understanding to concrete decisions on spe- cific issues. A constricted methodology would be one falling into either one or both of the following errors. It might understand Christian ethics too narrowly; pertaining, for example, *only* to decision-making and action on particular moral issues and prob- lems, or pertaining *only* to the development of moral character. The notion of ethics itself would then fail to be sufficiently com- prehensive. Or a methodology might fail to designate the func- tion and authority of the Bible for *each* of the elements, even if the full spectrum of elements were present in the notion of ethics.

2. The other suggestion of high significance is that the role and authority of biblical materials might vary for the various elements of the Christian moral life. Materials appropriate for shaping self-understanding might be very different from those aiding decision-making on specific issues. Or the same materials might be used quite differently for different elements.

H. Edward Everding and Dana Wilbanks

The heart of Everding and Wilbanks' proposal for function- ally relating Christian ethics and the Bible is a process involv- ing four components: "the centrality of faith, images of God and human responsibility, communal context, and concrete re- sponse." [24] While it is not necessary for our present concerns to describe the proposed method in detail, enough must be sum- marized to supply a base for later comments.

The most helpful start might be to locate Everding and Wil- banks in light of descriptions offered earlier. Their understand- ing of Christian ethics belongs squarely to that of relational or response ethics, joining Curran and a host of others in seeing that model as the most fitting description of the Christian moral life. Indeed, in many ways their methodological proposal is the effort to say in detail how relational ethics understands the interaction of the Bible and ethics.

Everding and Wilbanks' objective is a double one: a) to *describe* how people, Christian and non-Christian alike, do in fact make decisions on moral matters; b) to *propose* a methodology for the functional interaction of Bible and ethics for the Christian life, a methodology that is in close keeping with the dynamics of the decision-making process as described. Each of the four key components discussed below is to be seen both generically (i.e., true for ethics as a general human enterprise) and with respect to Christian ethics in particular. The "particularity" of Christian ethics is to be seen, however, not in the distinctiveness of the components themselves—*formally* they are the same for everyone —but in the particular *content* given each component *for Christians*. This content is directly related to the place of the Bible in Christian ethics.

For Everding and Wilbanks, then, the model of relationality and responsibility describes not only the Christian moral life but the pattern of the moral life in general; and in each of the key components in that model the Bible is functionally related in a way that supplies important content specifically for Christian ethics. So while Christian ethics is, in its formal features, part of the shared human enterprise of ethics, there is nonetheless a very high place for biblical materials; indeed, the Bible is the major source of the distinctiveness Christian ethics can rightly claim.

What are the components of Everding and Wilbanks' methodology?

1. Faith is the core of ethics, whether biblical ethics, contem-

porary ethics, Christian ethics, or any ethics whatsoever. That is, each person has an object (or objects) of ultimate trust, loyalty and commitment. Thus he or she has "faith" in something or someone. This object functions as a deity. People, in different words, all have a center of faith and this faith-relation is for each the crucial determinant in shaping ethical style, judgment and action. The self's direction and orientation is a consequence of its "faith." [25]

Everding and Wilbanks' claim is that this accurately describes the self in decision-making. It is generically true, however varied in kind and content the particular objects of trust, or however varied the centers of value people hold.

In form, the foregoing outline describes the function of faith in the biblical communities as well as in any and all others. This, however, does not specify the particular claim and content of the *specific* faith of the biblical communities. That claim is that there is one true God, the only God worthy of love and trust and the only God who can bring creation to fulfillment. The content of this faith is mediated through a particular set of images of this God and of fitting human response to his activity.

The mention of images introduces the second of the four "integrative ingredients" [26] in Everding and Wilbanks' methodology.

2. Formally, images function in the same way for all people, whatever their object of trust and concern. They are the media through which the self sees the world, interprets what is going on in any given situation, and formulates a response in keeping with what is seen and understood.

The content of ethics will vary from one person to another, from one community and culture to another, even within the life of the same person, in accord with differences among the dominating images. For *Christian* ethics in particular, the decisive place of the Bible is in its claim that the true center of faith is God and in its particular "imagistic" presentation of this God, his activity, and human response and responsibility. These biblical images supply the biblical content which the self may appropriate for its ethics. They mediate the content of faith in the ultimate object of the Christian moral life, God in Christ.

Several important points are to be made about biblical imagery.

a) Biblical images are not the same as general themes or motifs or ideas. These may be legitimate and helpful abstractions *from* images. But they must not be confused with images, which might best be defined as "vivid pictures" and which lead a richer life than any abstractions from them." [27]

b) Biblical imagery, the constellation of these vivid pictures, "is richly variegated, radically pluralistic, and even conflictual." [28] Any attempt to harmonize or systematize them all, or choose only one image, in order to provide an abstracted body of content for theology and ethics will inevitably do violence to the Bible's richness in pointing to God. In fact, for Everding and Wilbanks one of the chief tasks of exegesis is to protect the myriad character of biblical images as a kind of collage.[29] Their conviction here is in keeping with Curran's that a plurality of understandings of the moral life exists in scripture and any attempt to develop a single systematic biblical morality is unbiblical.[30]

c) The function of the biblical images for ethics, in keeping with the functions of images in general, is to provide "a window to the world that shapes the self's interpretations of situations and, thereby, his decisions." [31] Through its imagery, the Bible helps form the self's moral vision. Or, in Curran's words, the biblical images help forge the Christian's stance, horizon, or posture, his or her orientation to the world. For both Curran and Everding and Wilbanks this role and function of the Bible is *the* decisive one for Christian ethics.

d) The appropriateness of different biblical images for different situations becomes an important concern for ethics. Everding and Wilbanks note, "it is not likely that the 'warrior' image will illumine the question of abortion, nor is it likely the 'kindly father' image will illumine the situation of 'the wretched of the earth.' " [32] The methodological question then becomes that of the criteria for determining the appropriateness of varied images. This is addressed in several ways, some of them taken up later in our discussion. For the moment it is important simply to register the fact that this appropriateness entails determinants imposed *both* by the biblical materials *and* by the present decision-situation. Faithfulness to the text and "fittingness" of the image for the canon as a whole would be examples of the former, the power of the image to illumine the situation and decision at hand would be an example of the latter.

3. The third integrative ingredient is "the communal context in which the self experiences a dialogic relation of Bible and situation." [33] The single most crucial community for *Christian* ethics is the church since it is the community that "represents a continuing responsiveness both to biblical tradition and to contemporary situations." [34] It is composed of those who profess the same center of faith and share the biblical images of God's activity and human responsibility. It is, in a word, the ongoing community that works at functionally relating Bible and ethics in an ongoing way.

Everding and Wilbanks are quick to point out the influence of other communities that together with the church comprise the communal context that shapes the self and provides the materials for making, evaluating and acting upon decisions. This strong influence of multiple communities means, among other things, that Christian ethics must work out the inter-relationship of biblical images and contemporary cultural images. It means, too, that Christian ethics will involve sources of information and insight that are non-biblical and non-ecclesiastical.

In any case, the self becomes, decides, and acts in *community*. This is true for Christian and non-Christian alike. The communal context is always a critical component for ethics. The location of the self matters immensely for the shaping of its morality.

For Christian ethics in particular, the church has special responsibilities as the community that functionally relates the Bible and ethics. It is responsible for

> the evaluation and selection of biblical images, the manner in which biblical images are appropriated in contemporary situations and the manner in which contemporary situations affect biblical interpretation. . . .[35]

The place of the church is a subject to which we shall turn later.

4. The final ingredient is concrete response. Just as the biblical communities, by way of formulations such as laws, codes and teachings, made specific and precise their perceptions of faithfulness in concrete historical situations, so, too, for us concrete response is integral to relating Bible and ethics. The relationship is not consummated until we have given concrete expression to our understanding of the meaning of faithfulness in and for our particular setting. Biblical materials themselves are not truly appropriated until the Christian has taken a stand and acted upon this issue and that. Relating the Bible and Christian ethics is an enterprise "historical" in the extreme.[36]

These four ingredients—the centrality of faith, images of God and human responsibility, communal context and concrete response—are the components of Everding and Wilbanks' proposed methodology. Although we have treated them in skeletal fashion, it should be evident that Everding and Wilbanks have introduced elements important to the concerns of this volume. We shall return to the substance of these in later chapters.[37]

Brevard S. Childs

Although a number of biblical scholars have attempted to apply their work to particular ethical issues, Brevard Childs is one of the few who has directly addressed the methodological questions about the relationship between the Bible and ethical decision-making. He devotes a helpful chapter to this subject in his book *Biblical Theology in Crisis*.[38]

1. Childs approaches the matter from within the context of faith, as would any Christian facing an ethical issue, and he reminds us that from within that context the central task is not the objective understanding of the Bible's ethical passages but the discernment of God's will. "The issue turns on the question to what extent God's will has been made clear and unequivocal for his people." [39]

Throughout history the church has claimed God's Word in the scriptures as a primary source for knowing God's will. Childs points to a fundamental tension that lies both within the scriptures themselves and in the situation of modern Christians seeking to know God's will for their lives. On the one hand the Bible speaks often of the understanding that God's will has been made known. Numerous passages speak of the imperatives which state what is required for the obedient life. Thus, both Jesus and the prophets could castigate those who had failed to live out those imperatives. On the other hand the Old and the New Testaments also speak of a living God whose will is constantly being revealed anew in relationship to his people in concrete situations and particular individuals. Although his will has been made known God has also given his people the responsibility of freedom to discern that will in every new present. "At no point within the Bible is there ever spelled out a system or a technique by which one could move from the general imperatives of the law of God, such as found in the Decalogue, to the specific application within the concrete situation." [40]

The tension in which the Christian decision-maker stands is very much like this. He believes that God's will has been made known in the scripture and tradition, but he also knows that this does not relieve him of the struggle to discover that will anew in the present concrete situation. Childs suggests that, as in the biblical understanding, the knowing of God's will cannot emerge apart from doing it. God's will becomes clear only in the midst of our involvement in his work.

2. Having established the will of God as a focal point Childs turns his attention to the process of seeking biblical warrants for making ethical decisions. He begins by reminding us of the central importance of the formation of the canon. This is perhaps Childs' most distinctive contribution to the discussion. The biblical canon represents the judgment of the community of believers that the entire body of scripture is to be considered as authoritatively revealing the will of God. This provides a tremendous corrective to the way the Bible is often used in ethical matters. We are not free to engage in isolated passages to support a point. A more disciplined process will be necessary. Childs indicates a process of first discovering the full range of witnesses within the

canon on a given issue and then seeking to understand the inner relationships between these witnesses. This wider canonical perspective would put an end to the sort of proof-texting approach that seems to go on in even the most sophisticated ethical works. It would also put new emphasis on the Bible as the church's book. "The context of the canon serves to remind its users that the Bible does not function as Scriptures apart from the community of believers." [41] It also shows the ongoingness of God's activity as a living God, implying that contemporary Christians should expect that activity to still be present in ever new forms and not frozen for consultation in the record of the biblical past.

3. In seeking specific warrants for an ethical decision Childs stresses the possibility that within the canon one may well find a great variety of approaches to an issue. It is then necessary to understand the different historical circumstances which called these approaches forth, and to determine their inner relationship within the canon. He cites as an example the tremendous pluralism on questions of sexual relationship represented by Genesis 2; the Song of Songs; Proverbs 7; Leviticus 19; 1 Corinthians 7 and 1 Peter 3.[42] No one of these diverse passages could be taken as the final word on the subject. One must also be prepared to discover that there are important ethical questions which the Bible does not address at all. This must be acknowledged without attempting to read into the text meanings that are not there.

There is, Childs stresses, no one type of warrant for ethical decision to be found in the Bible. One might find a clear imperative, or a tension between the poles of two conflicting approaches, or sets of priorities and options depending on persons and circumstances. These then can provide resources for moving from deciding to acting. An imperative like "You shall love your neighbor as yourself" becomes in Jesus' teaching ("Who then is my neighbor?") the substance of a fresh imperative that impels us to seek the neighbor in our own situation. When the biblical warrants provide us with opposite poles on a question then a responsible decision must take account of the emphases being made by each approach and their relation to one another. For example, the attitudes toward sexual relationship displayed in Proverbs 7 and in the Song of Songs are at quite opposite ends of the spectrum. A biblical view of sexual ethics must somehow stand within the tension created by this polarity of viewpoint.[43] The biblical warrants might provide us with a wide range of options no one of which is advanced as *the* responsible alternative. In Paul's famous advice to the Corinthians he urges that it would be best not to marry, but better to marry than to be aflame with passion (1 Cor. 7). On some issues a wide range of alternatives may appear, but these then serve to establish the boundaries within which the church's efforts to seek the responsible decision must take place. To discover such options within the biblical warrants emphasizes that wide differences of opinion within the Christian community may rightly claim some biblical foundation, but where the range of alternatives is broad no one group can claim absolute authority. A proper understanding of the biblical warrants at this point will help to hold dissent on ethical issues within the church where moral debate can take place in an atmosphere of Christian community rather than between opposing camps of moral self-righteousness.

Childs' plea is finally for a recognition of the multiplicity of models for biblical warrants in decision-making. "It is obviously a mistake to approach every issue with only one biblical model in mind. Many a pastor had decided on a question of social ethics in the spirit of Paul before Agrippa or Luther before the Emperor, when the issue was one which called for compromise after the manner of the sage in Proverbs." [44] The church must diligently seek out the full range of biblical warrants and then faithfully enter the dialog with them in full awareness of the present circumstances within which moral decisions must be made.

One can only be grateful to Childs for his insight into the character of biblical material as it relates to ethical decision. This is an area of tremendous misunderstanding in the church. One can only regret that circumstances dictated only one brief chapter on the subject. Many of Childs' insights need fuller treatment. For example, much needed is a fuller discussion of the relationship between church and canon and the implications of this relationship for our use of the Bible. Also because of space limitations a number of issues were either explicitly set aside or simply not treated. One wonders how the use of critical method in biblical study might fit into Childs' picture. Certainly a full discovery of the time-conditioned character of biblical accounts would reinforce the care with which one seeks biblical warrants for present action. To what extent does this affect the authority of biblical warrants? In fact, the general question of biblical authority is one that must be addressed more directly, especially in light of the wider canonical context which Childs urges. Particularly urgent is the question of the relationship between biblical authority and the authority of non-biblical resources. For example, the discussion of homosexuality in many denominations has presented an issue in which biblical warrants often seem to conflict directly with positions based on more recent non-biblical insights. Finally, Childs' discussion certainly provokes many thoughts on implications for the local congregation in its efforts to make the Bible a usable resource. How would a congregation prepare itself for the active use of the Bible in Christian decision-making? We must return to these issues at a later point.

C. Freeman Sleeper

C. Freeman Sleeper is another biblical scholar whose writing merits special attention. The title of the essay concerned, which appears in two versions, suggests Sleeper's proposal for the relating of Bible and ethics: "Ethics As a Context for Biblical Interpretation." [45] The "ethics" Sleeper has in mind is not the ethics of the biblical communities, however, but the ethics of present-day communities in which Christians participate. More accurately, Sleeper seeks contemporary moral issues and decision-making situations in our social and political life as providing "a vital context, if not the most important context, for pursuing biblical studies." [46] His prime purpose is to develop a different style of biblical studies and he sees current issues and situations as the medium for this new approach. He also contends that biblical materials will occupy a vital place in addressing those very moral issues and decision-situations that are the context for this style of biblical studies. There is a necessary conversation, then, between biblical scholars and Christian ethicists and Sleeper proposes a particular method as the set of common terms with which this conversation can get underway.

The question of hermeneutics, or interpretation, is Sleeper's organizing scheme for this method.

> The interpretation of the Bible is not essentially different from that of any other document. That is to say, all interpretation is the task of trying to understand, in one social and cultural setting, symbols which originated in a different context. . . . Furthermore, all interpretation involves three stages. First, it depends on *how we see,* on such factors as the extent and kind of our technical training, or our personal skill in picking up clues. This first stage is what I choose to call *perspective.* The second

stage depends on *what we see;* it focuses on the *sources* which we are studying, on the way in which they are presented or preserved. Finally, interpretation involves *how we express what we saw,* or the stage of *communication.* Biblical interpretation shares these general features of all other historical interpretation. . . .[47]

Most of Sleeper's essay is an explication of each of these three stages and their meaning for his own guild of biblical scholars and its pursuit of biblical studies. Our discussion will extract only what is directly pertinent to later chapters of this volume.

1. The first stage of interpretation, "how we see" or "perspective" is of first-rate importance for any methodology, a matter we have already noted. Here we only underline, as does Sleeper, the role of "pre-understanding" (Bultmann) in our approach to *both* the biblical materials *and* the decision-situation at hand. For both Bible and ethics the task of clarifying our perspectives, of being self-conscious about the bundle of biases, convictions and assumptions we possess, is a methodological imperative because of the heavy interpreting influence of our outlooks.

2. Sleeper's comments about the second stage, "what we see" or "sources," are significant for us at the point of his characterization of biblical language. The *way* in which the sources are preserved and presented matters. The *forms* of keeping and passing on shape to no small degree what we see and hear. "Images, symbols and myths" are the terms Sleeper uses to describe the particular language forms of the biblical materials. Whether these are the best choices is not the concern at the moment. Rather, it is that the form of presentation makes a difference for the way we see things and respond to them.

Two items of conjecture might be advanced here, even though

they do not belong in an explicit way to Sleeper's presentation. It might be conjectured that some forms of discourse (such as images, symbols, and metaphors) exercise more influence on the shaping of people's morality than other forms (such as rational concepts of right and wrong or the instructional language of rules, principles, and maxims). And/or it might be contended that some forms of discourse are more influential at certain points in the shaping of morality (such as image and symbol for the development of character and the cultivation of moral sensibilities), while other forms are more influential at other points (such as concepts and rational discourse for deliberating about specific policies and actions).

We can put this discussion aside for now, noting for later consideration that because the Bible clearly does employ a wide variety of language forms, how they are related to the shaping of morality is an important methodological concern.

3. Sleeper describes the third stage, "how we express what we saw" or "communication," as consisting of three elements that span the distance between the biblical materials and the present. The position taken is so close to Everding and Wilbanks' that we need only outline it as a way of bringing to the fore issues earlier tagged as important.

• There is a dialog in the communication stage between biblical images and contemporary secular images. (This raises again the methodological question of the relationship of biblical and non-biblical sources in ethics, and their respective authority.)

• There is also a dialog between biblical images and prevailing "models" in the social sciences, their representations of societal dynamics. (This raises much the same methodological question.)

• There is the meaning of biblical images for present-day

Christian ethical theory itself. Here Sleeper joins Everding and Wilbanks, Curran and others in saying that the Bible's contribution to ethical theory is not that of providing a distinctive theory of its own but that of supplying "peculiar and important insights into the nature of human responsibility. . . ." [48]

Sleeper concludes his discussion of the third stage with a cataloging of "what communication does *not* mean" in the use of the Bible for Christian ethics. It is a very helpful list, and we use it to close this discussion. [49]

> . . . First, we should not try to find biblical *strategies or solutions* to modern problems. . . . Attempts to find 'the biblical answer' by an appeal to prooftexts is simply wrong because the Bible did not anticipate many contemporary issues, because there is development within the Bible itself, and because the biblical solutions are historically conditioned. By itself, the Bible cannot tell us what to do. We must also draw on other insights from the Christian tradition, on other sources of secular wisdom, and on relevant technical information. . . .

> . . . Second, we should *not* try to find *parallels* between our own situation and that of the biblical writers in order that the Bible might 'speak to us.' It is no doubt true that communication is easier where there are such parallels, as in the case of Christians who are being persecuted or suppressed, but in most cases this requirement would mean that the Bible is simply irrelevant.

> . . . Third, we should *not* try to extrapolate from the Bible *only one ethical norm*—the polarity of law and gospel (or gospel and law); love (whether as a transcendent or as a situational norm); the imitation of Christ; the

Kingdom of God; natural law. All of these, and many others, have been used to illuminate Christian decision-making. However, by reducing Christian ethics to a single norm, other important aspects of biblical ethical reflection are neglected. Since our task is to communicate the biblical message faithfully rather than literally, we should insist on an ethical perspective comprehensive enough to include all of the central and distinctive biblical insights.

*   *   *   *   *

This review of recent and current work of biblical scholars and Christian ethicists has raised many questions that will need to be addressed in any constructive statement about the use of the Bible in Christian ethics. We conclude this chapter by clustering these questions in four groups that serve to introduce the remainder of the book and to signal the content of our own proposal for relating the Bible and ethics. When we have addressed these matters, we will have met the purpose of this volume.

1. Any comprehensive methodology for relating the Bible and Christian ethics needs to make clear what it understands as belonging to Christian ethics. What is its range of concern, its field of investigation? What different realities are its subjects? What are the categories that might be used to carry on its work?

When Christian ethics has made explicit the various elements or dimensions of the moral life with which it is concerned, it remains to be said how the Bible relates to each of them. At what specific points and places in the Christian moral life do biblical materials have an appropriate and influential impact? Where and toward what ends do we employ scripture? Do the kinds or types of appropriate biblical materials vary from one point or place to another? Can something be said about the nature of the influence?

What is the proper starting point in relating Bible and ethics? Does one begin with the biblical materials or with the situation demanding of a response to some moral issue or problem? What difference does the starting point make? Are there different starting points for different elements of the moral life?

2. The place of the church for the functional relating of Bible and ethics must be addressed. What are the tasks of the church as a community of moral formation and of moral deliberation? At what points in the life of the church is the Bible brought to bear upon these? How does the church as a context affect the practical relating of the Bible to ethical issues? Is the church a necessary context for this?

3. What is the authority of the Bible in making moral judgments? This question is best focused by asking, how and to what extent is scripture the revealing of God's will? Does God continue to reveal himself? If so, how authoritative are non-biblical sources of insight? Does the authority of scripture have a different character than that of other sources? What is their relation? What are the controls which prevent each individual from choosing among biblical and non-biblical sources in accord with convictions already held?

4. A critical point for an adequate methodology is to clearly understand the nature of the resources to be found in the Bible and how one must go about making those resources available to the church in dealing with modern ethical issues. What kind of exegesis is appropriate to this task? How important is the original form and context of biblical materials? Are all biblical materials equally important? How do we choose among the bewildering

variety of viewpoints in the scripture? Are there controls on our choosing? Is analogy an appropriate technique in measuring biblical passages against modern situations? What is the relationship of one biblical reference to the whole of scripture? Does this make a difference? Does the nature of different biblical resources already suggest different ways in which they might relate to moral life? If so, what are these ways?

3 understanding the task of christian ethics

In the previous chapter we referred to the matter of comprehensiveness in methodology.[1] That is taken up again now in order to state as lucidly and succinctly as we can something of the nature and tasks of Christian ethics. When one "does" Christian ethics, what does one "do"? What is the range of its inquiry and analysis, its field of investigation? What are the realities it seeks to describe and assess? What categories are useful for its work? And how and where do biblical materials function?

Charles Curran's previously cited remark initiates our discussion.

> . . . Some methodological approaches to Christian ethics appear to be erroneous precisely because they fail to consider all the elements that should enter into the ethical consideration. Perhaps no mention is made of the decision process itself, or the attitudes and dispositions of the subject, or the values and goals in the Christian life. In general, an ethical approach must try to be as com-

prehensive as possible by considering all the elements that go into ethical considerations even though some will obviously have priority and be of greater importance.[2]

What are ". . . the elements that go into ethical considerations. . . . ?" Can we say which "have priority and [are] of greater importance?" Can we designate the place of scripture in the answers to these questions?

We can begin by identifying the chief subject of these pages, the self and the choices and actions it makes and undertakes. What is the significance of the self and its formation for the moral life? What is the relationship of this formation to specific decisions and actions? How does who we are affect what we do, and *vice versa?* And what particular concerns of its own does Christian ethics bring to these matters?

The various categories employed in our discussion will be directed toward these and related questions.

The nature of these categories needs to be underlined at the outset. They are all *formal* categories. That is, even while the *content* of each of them may vary from one morality to the next, *structurally* (or "formally") they remain the same throughout. They belong to ethics *as ethics,* whether Christian ethics, Moslem ethics, Hindu ethics, some secular humanist ethics, or whatever. Insofar as we may occasionally use them with reference to a specific content, we will do so for Christian ethics in particular. For the major portion of this chapter, however, we use them as the descriptive and analytical tools of ethics as a general enterprise.

The scheme for addressing this subject of the self and its decisions can be depicted visually as follows.

CHARACTER FORMATION	DECISION-MAKING AND ACTION
the good person	the right action
moral value	moral obligation
the ethics of being	the ethics of doing

The solid line represents the unbroken connection between *the formation of the self and its concrete decisions and actions.* The broken perpendicular line indicates that these two main subjects are not to be thought of as separated from one another in reality even though we do so tentatively for the sake of discussion.

To begin with we shall name only the major categories and elements for each column. Further distinctions can be added later.

Ethics has used several different phrases to discuss the substance of these two columns. The attention to the first—character or identity—is the focus of one of the ancient and persistent questions of ethics, "who is the good person." Or, if the reference is to *corporate* identity or character, "what is the good community or the good society." *Traits of character or qualities of being* are the subject for ethical inquiry and judgment here. The reality investigated and assessed is *the kind of person* the decision-maker is. Attention is to "the ethics of being," to those elements in the moral life we sometimes say reside within the person— motives, dispositions, intentions and attitudes, for example. Judgments made about such elements will be *judgments of moral value,* judgments about what traits or qualities ought to characterize the good person or community. The overriding concern is simply who we are and ought to be as persons or groups of persons.

For the second subject—decision-making and action—the focus is that of another ancient and persistent question of ethics, "what is right action." (Or, "what ought I or we to do.") *Concrete choices and deeds in particular circumstances* on specific moral issues and problems are the subject of ethical inquiry and judgment. The reality investigated and assessed is the process of decision-making, as well as the rightness and wrongness of the particular decisions and actions chosen or considered. Attention is directed to "the ethics of doing," to those elements in the moral life which we view as extending from us—the deliberation with others and then the action itself. Judgments made about these elements will be *judgments of moral obligation,* judgments about what it is we are morally obliged to do.

These are some of the terms and categories used to help think about important realities in the moral life: moral value/moral obligation, the ethics of being/the ethics of doing, the good person/the right action.

Expanding our list to include categories that designate the *tasks* of Christian ethics, we can identify the following: a descriptive task, a critical task, and a normative task. The first seeks simply to comprehend and describe the moral life as it is actually lived. The second makes critical inquiry about it. The third attempts to state the proper content and procedures for living it as it ought to be lived.

The descriptive task covers a number of different concerns. How in fact do people make ethical choices and what are the qualities of character which they embody? What are the operative creeds and the moralities by which they live? What moral justification (or supportive reasons) do they give for their decisions and actions? Critical assessment, the second task, follows: what is to be made of this way of being and doing, these creeds and moralities, this set of justifying reasons? Do they hold up in the light of critical reflection? Is this faith and morality worthy of the allegiance invested in them? Is this justification faulty or sound? Are the specific choices and actions taken faulty or sound?

These two tasks of description and assessment are often encompassed by the term "critical ethics," a term we shall use in the pages that follow.

The third task, belonging to what is often called "normative" or "constructive" ethics, is that of providing recommended content and method for the moral life and supplying sound supporting reasons for these. Normative ethics attempts to say what the good life is, what characterizes the good person and the good society, what marks the right decision and action on a particular matter. It attempts to say, too, which means and procedures and structures will realize this content. It seeks to designate right norms and criteria and state how ethical decision-making itself ought to proceed. And for all of this, normative ethics attempts to give defensible rationale, sound reasons subject to public scrutiny.

Further questions arise, many of them internal to the work of ethics itself. What are its own procedures for description of the moral life? What are its standards and its tools for critical assessment? What are the sources and norms for its constructive task? Yet for our purposes the above distinctions among the tasks of ethics, and some awareness of the line of questioning that ethics entails, will suffice. With these and the other categories in hand we can turn to the subject of the self, its decisions and actions.

The Nature and Significance of Character

Most of the writing in American Christian ethics in this century has been preoccupied with decision-making and action on specific moral problems and issues. In both common parlance and in the literature, "ethics" as a term has become virtually synonymous with arriving at stands and advocating responses on a particular moral matter, whether abortion, fetal research, euthanasia, homosexuality, race or sex discrimination, the Indochina war, food aid policy, the exercise of governmental power, or whatever. In different words, Christian ethics has been issue- or problem-oriented ethics. Its focus has been on decision-making and action.

At the same time, however, a considerable body of literature has grown up on the subject of moral development, the forming of moral character. The sources have been chiefly psychology and other behavioral sciences and writers in Christian ethics have drawn increasingly upon these. In fact, the focus upon character has recently become a major one in both Protestant and Catholic ethics in the U.S.[3] Character formation is our subject here as well, although the attention will be given less to the psychological dynamics than to the significance of character formation for the moral life. Our contention is that this traditionally neglected topic in American Christian ethics is also the most important one. It should have higher priority and be considered of greater importance than has been the case. Our contention is also that biblical materials can and ought to exercise their greatest impact upon Christian ethics at this point; that is, upon the character or the identity of the decision-maker.

But this is anticipating later discussions. What about the subject at hand, the formation and the significance of character for morality?

Character is formed by social processes in a constant "conversation" that goes on between self and society. Multiple elements are involved—sex, race, class, nationality, cultural heritage, religious experience, ideological persuasion, family and institutional patterns, particular events and traditions, as well as accompanying frameworks of meaning and interpretation. These elements in various constellations compose that dynamic and complex reality we call "society." Society provides a certain world—this one and not that one—to develop the identity of those who inhabit it. Identity development occurs along with the appropriation by the self of that particular world. The self is thus radically dependent upon its social world. Without it he or she would not "be" as a self. The self may well change settings, move to and among different environs, but it cannot either be formed or function apart from the concrete particulars of the social world it inhabits.

At the same time the self fashions the various elements of its social world together in its own way. While the sources and substance of the person's history and experience are located in his or her social world, they are "worked upon" by the person in such a way as to become genuinely his or her own rendering of them. The self orders the various elements and their meanings into a pattern of configuration that makes the self itself and not some other self.

The self does more than fashion what it inherits and experiences, however. It injects what it has fashioned "back into" society. Its own subjective meanings, and the way of life that expresses them, then become *part of* society, part of the very elements and the frameworks of meaning by which the self becomes. These subjective meanings and their embodiments become part of the patterns of life, including institutional life, in such a way that they take on an objective or public character, a life outside the self.

There is, then, a genuine interaction and interdependence of the self and its social world. In a certain sense they are twin-born. The self simply would not "be" apart from its social world. Yet it fashions the materials in a way unique to itself. And in one way or another, to one degree or another, it also has its own creative influence upon its particular social world.

The salient point for our concerns is that the formation of character or identity is a dialogic process in community. Neither the human self nor its social world lives without the other. The particular character of each deeply affects the other.

Identity or character is, then, a designation for the particular "being" of a person as that has been and continues to be forged from many social factors into the personality constellation distinctive of that person. It designates the special configuration of self that makes me me and not someone else.[4]

This does not yet indicate the significance of character for the moral life. What is the moral import of identity? What is there in the nature and functioning of character that Christian ethics ought to take note of for its own concerns as ethics? We can discuss this as two topics, "faith and perception," and "perception, dispositions and intentions." Along the way we must ask what Christian ethics as ethics brings to these topics.

1. *Faith and perception.* At birth each of us enters a world already rich with constellations of meaning and experience. These are attached to various objects of human allegiance and trust, various human loves and loyalties, various human commitments. The objects might be those of religious devotion, or cultural heroes, a certain way of life, a nation or people, a cause or creed.

These objects of trust, love, loyalty and commitment signal

what is prized in the society. They represent what is regarded as of dominant value and overriding worth. They locate what the society deems as "the good" in accord with which life should be lived out.

Functionally the objects of trust and commitment "order" society. The priorities among them are the priorities of the society. The rest is given its place and status around them. The many elements we mentioned above—race, sex, class, etc.—are assigned their slot and significance in the social world in accord with the dominating human allegiances and commitments present in any given time and place. In a word, our lives take shape in keeping with our functional deities (the objects of most basic trust and loyalty). And our social world is already alive with these "gods" as we enter it.

The social world is also already alive with myriad forms of human communication—stories, images, symbols, historical accounts, traditions and rituals, paradigms, myths, rational discourse and instruction, beliefs and creeds, metaphors and allegories, visions and dreams. These multiple forms carry the meanings attached to the objects of human devotion and commitment. They are the means of presenting what it is the "gods" have to say. They are the media for conveying what life in this time and place is about and how it is to be lived out. Knowing the social world into which we are born is knowing its dominating objects of love and loyalty; it is simultaneously knowing the dominating images, stories, symbols and traditions that capture and express what these objects mean.

A very large part of character formation is the internalizing by the self of some (never all) of the objects of human trust and loyalty in the self's particular social world. It is also the simultaneous internalizing of the images and tales and recounted histories that belong with these objects. This internalization means that *particular* objects of trust, real or imagined, become those of the self and its devotion, along with the *particular* content of the accompanying images and symbols and paradigms. The self's character or identity is shaped in accord with these objects and these images. They now order its world, they "read" events and experience and assign meanings in keeping with the self's dominant commitments. They comprise the priorities in the self's own history and yield coherence and continuity as the self moves from situation to situation and experience to experience.

Most important for our present concern is this: the internalization of the "gods" and the internalization of what they have to say shapes *the way the self sees the world, thinks about it, and responds to it.* Perception, awareness, reflection, and conduct are all tied inextricably to the *particular* objects of trust and love and commitment we have made our own and to the *particular* forms of presentation of their content we have adopted as genuinely ours.[5]

Recalling Everding and Wilbanks' discussion,[6] we can use the word "faith" to indicate *both* the fact of having dominant objects of trust and centers of value *and* the content that results from having this or that particular set of loves and loyalties. A person thus both "has faith" (in something or other) and has "a faith" (a belief system by which his or her life is ordered). Adding to this the notion of "perception" as the self's way of seeing things (its general perspective on life, its angle of vision), we can begin to draw out the import of character for the moral life. That might be expressed as follows.

Who we are and are becoming as a result of the faith we hold determines in large part *what we see.* So much so that two people with differing character may see the same event very differently and respond accordingly in dissimilar ways. Here seeing is far more than observation. It is interpretation and valuing. Some horizons become the horizons of the self's interests, some do not. Some matters are regarded as worthy of response, some are not. Some fall within the range of vision, some do not. Some are deemed morally significant and some are not—and not a few fail to occur to us as moral matters at all, even while our next door neighbor regards them as issues of the first order. It all depends upon our "view" of things.

The relationship of faith and perception can be stated in another way. "What people define as real is real in its consequences" is an accepted axiom in the social sciences. The pictures of reality we hold, whether around particular events or in general, are determinants of our behavior. How we "define" things sets the direction and limits of our conduct, generating certain choices and activities rather than others, underlining some issues as *the* moral issues rather than others, disposing us to a particular kind of response and not another one. Why we do one thing and not another, indeed why we do something instead of nothing at all, depends upon our apprehension of things. At the end of our responses dangle our views of the world.

The matter underlined here is that what we "define as real" is an outcome of who we are; our picture of things is expressive of our particular identity or character. That in turn is expressive of the tangle of loves and loyalties and commitments that comprise the faith we live by. We see and act in accord with the "definitions" of reality that our faith evokes. Believing is seeing!

The moral significance of character resides in part then in the fact that our "being" shapes our "seeing" and the way we see things gives us a particular outlook and orientation toward life. This in turn disposes us to take seriously certain kinds of concerns and activities and not others, to regard one set of matters as important and not another, to include some horizons within the reality of our world and not others. Perception thus sets the boun-

daries and the general course of our conduct on moral matters
and it "in-forms" the choices and actions we make and undertake. Some choices are attractive and compelling, some are repul-
sive. And some choices for others never occur to us as choices
at all. We just don't see things that way. In the words of a Chi-
nese proverb: "Ninety percent of what we see lies *behind* our
eyes."

It is difficult to exaggerate the significance of perception. Few
factors explain so much of our behavior as the simple fact that
we are different people who see things differently. It is equally
difficult to exaggerate the importance, not just of "faith" as a
phenomenon, but *which* objects of faith and *which* images and
stories are internalized so as to shape our vision in a particular
way.

It is appropriate to pause here and ask what questions and
concerns Christian ethics as critical and normative ethics would
bring to the description thus far. We can focus upon the subject
of faith.

As indicated, the faith (or the faiths) held by the self and its
communities locates "the good" in accord with which life is to
be lived out. The objects found ultimately worthwhile and trust-
worthy, deserving of the self's allegiance, devotion and attach-
ment, are the objects that function as the sources and content of
moral goodness. They tell us what our conduct ought to conform to, that from which our living and dying should take its
clues. They embody what is regarded as of dominant value and
importance, the priorities for a way of life. They constitute "the
good" for the self.

Critical Christian ethics will want to ask not only what these
objects of ultimate concern are, in actual fact, and what their
behavioral effect is in the life of the "believer." It will also want
to ask whether their status as objects of basic and final trust and

commitment is one of which they are deserving. Are they, in different words, truly the gods or God? Or are they relative "goods" granted the power and status of absolute "goods?" Are they idols or not?Should or should not the self or community live out its life under their banner and command and take its marching orders from them? Are they truly *"the* good?"

Normative ethics will want to describe, commend and justify a particular understanding of the source and nature of the good. For Christian ethics in particular, this will entail a faith claim that God in Christ is the final source of moral goodness and the object of ultimate trust, love, loyalty and commitment. There will be other "goods," to be sure, but they will take their (relative) places in accord with the will of God as the central defining ethical content. (There will also be multiple understandings of the nature of God in Christ, of the will of God, and the meaning of that for the moral life. These are matters encompassed by *theological ethics* as part of the larger enterprise of Christian ethics.)

Critical ethics will, as part of its concern for locating "the good" which faith defines, also want to disclose and appraise the images, stories, traditions, rituals, symbols, and the other media of faith that so shape perception. Normative or constructive ethics will want to commend and defend certain of these and their meanings as that which ought to shape our way of looking at life and responding to it. Christian ethics thus will insist that in one way or another the basic events and symbols and stories in the Christian faith will be defining of goodness in the moral life—the creation accounts; the exodus narrative; the prophetic corpus; the life, death, resurrection and teachings of Jesus; the hope and vision of things to come; to list examples. While again there is room for considerable variety in the understanding of the Christian faith, it is nonetheless inevitable that when

Christian ethics undertakes its task as normative ethics it must spell out the meaning of the faith and its presentation for the moral life. (Doing that means Christian ethics will be choosing or constructing some particular normative understanding of the faith itself. Here again Christian ethics becomes a close conversation partner with theology.)

We can return now to our description of the self in the moral life, having taken note of the kinds of concerns Christian ethics brings to the subject of faith.

2. Perception, Dispositions, and Intentions. We can give some precision to the place of character in the moral life by discussing the function of dispositions and intentions and their relation to perception.

Dispositions are those elements of our character we can call simply our "persisting attitudes." For the sake of example, let us say that our conduct is regularly marked by hopefulness and compassion in some domains of life and cynicism and disdain in others. When these or some other sets of attitudes are not simply episodic but carry over from situation to situation and experience to experience we become "disposed" to this pattern of response rather than another one, we act and react in particular and relatively consistent ways. We develop certain habits or habitual patterns in the moral life and these provide some moral continuity as we move from one decision-situation to another. In fact the habits may become so strong and "natural" to us that many of our decisions themselves are no longer made in a self-conscious way. We just "intuit" or "know" how to respond without ever asking a question like, "What do I believe in and what does that mean for the matter at hand?"

Dispositions flow from the overarching orientation or vision that informs them. They are in keeping with the way we see life. They are the attitudinal expressions of our perception that "dispose" us to prefer one kind of choice over another and act in one manner rather than another.

Intentions are also in keeping with the general posture toward life expressive of our identity. They are in character, too, with our dispositions. But intentions are distinct from dispositions in that they signal a deliberately chosen or self-conscious activity, a volitional activity that "attitudes" as a notion does not convey. Intentions are closely associated with willing, with purposive, goal-oriented determinations. We self-consciously "intend" to achieve a certain goal or become a certain kind of person, realize a particular end or avoid a particular fate, act in line with a certain ideal or basic conviction.

Like dispositions, intentions ward off atomism in the moral life by supplying a coherence for the self as it moves from one decision-situation to another. Consecutive and even distantly separated choices and actions line up with, or cohere around, our intentions. This provides direction in our deciding and doing. Our choices and acts are not wholly situation-determined, then; they are influenced and tied to one another by the set of intentions carried through various times and settings.

Perception, dispositions, and intentions—these are ways of describing elements of character that have considerable importance for the moral life. They set the boundaries and direction of our conduct, determine what is morally significant and what is not, and form the nature of our response to one situation after another. In conclusion, character is probably the chief architect of our decisions and actions. It fashions the self's moral landscape.

It is appropriate to pause again in our description and bring to bear the inquiries of critical and constructive ethics. We did so earlier for one of the persistent concerns of ethics, the nature and the location of "the good." We turn briefly now to the second area, the nature and character of the moral self.[7]

Critical Christian ethics will want to disclose and appraise the moral character or identity of a particular person or a community of people. What are its qualities and moral traits, its way of seeing things, its reigning dispositions and intentions? How do these hold up in the light of critical scrutiny? What case is to be made for them? Or against?

Constructive ethics will want to commend and defend a particular understanding or picture of who it is we should strive to be and become and how it is we might get there. Christian ethics will have its own say here as it seeks to describe the moral self normatively in light of the Christian faith. It will want to say which way of viewing life, which dispositions and which intentions, which values and which motives, are most in keeping with the faith. While again the latitude of plausible and legitimate understandings of Christian faith is sufficiently broad to allow considerable variety, Christian ethics cannot abstain from commending a particular perspective and way of life, at least in its broad outlines.

Decision-Making and Action

While character may be the chief architect of our choices and deeds, it is not the only major human reality in the moral life. Taking specific stands on concrete moral issues and acting in accord with the stands taken, these matters have their own dynamics for ethics, whatever their intimate ties to the character of the decision-maker. To answer the question, "who is the good person and what should be his or her bearing in this matter," (character) is not yet to answer the question, "what is the right course to take here" (decision-making and action). That requires further descriptions and considerations.

The moral life itself forces this further investigation and critique. Dispositions and intentions do not of themselves say *which* of several plausible choices and actions are most fulfilling of the governing intentions and most in keeping with the reigning dispositions. Several possible courses may appear in character with the person of the decision-maker. Indeed, *all* considered may be in character in one way or another, to one degree or another. Yet not all conceivable choices and actions can be undertaken or all potentialities of character realized. Multiple limitations of various sorts impinge. Some judgment must be made about the course most fitting under the circumstances, the action most appropriate in this time and place on this particular issue. The finite constraints of the moral life itself thus force a specificity of choice and action which dispositions and intentions do not of themselves supply. So even when we have clarified for ourselves what it is we intend to achieve and even when we know what attitudes we desire to characterize our efforts, we face still further questions about what it is that is to be done. What data is to be marshalled and regarded as significant? What factors and criteria are to be taken into account? What moral norms should be brought to bear? What process should be used for arriving at a decision?

A shift of attention has occurred here, one from "moral value" to "moral obligation." The concern now is for the basic principles, criteria and standards for determining the morally right thing to do, rather than the concern for what is morally good or bad as that applies to traits of personality or to persons and groups of people. This shift (to the second column in our diagram) is one we all make as we focus upon choices and actions. Ethics as a reflective enterprise simply discloses and holds up for analysis and assessment the various factors in the shift.

Before listing some of the ingredients of decision-making and action, we should mention that our concentration is on the former in this closely-knit pair. Action is not thereby relegated to a place of lesser importance. Without it Christian ethics would be wholly without flesh. The emphasis on decision-making is explained by the fact that here we wish to highlight how the biblical materials might be enlisted.

What kinds of considerations regularly come to the fore as people make choices and seek to carry them out? Without any claim to an exhaustive or refined description, we mention the following as recognizable for most decisions.

1. In decision-making the person renders some analysis of the situation and the issues, some understanding of what is going on and what is significant there, what the critical issues and data are. He or she "defines what is real." This definition of what is occurring and what it means may be done carefully or impressionistically, and for recurring situations it may be assumed altogether. But it is present in any case. There is also at work some picture or model of society, how it actually functions and how it ought to.

2. Whether explicitly spelled out or not, some scheme or method for arriving at the right choice is present. Included are several elements, each of which could be elaborated in more detail than we can undertake here.

a) A way of proceeding, or a method of practical moral reasoning, is used. It supplies the steps for approaching and moving through a decision on some issue or problem. A common example is this one: "In order to decide, calculate as best you can the probable consequences of various courses of action and then weigh each in turn." As with other elements in the moral life the steps of reasoning on moral matters may become so habitual that on most decisions we give them little or no conscious consideration.

b) Norms or standards are always employed. As the word indicates, "norms" are the measures of "normative" conduct and procedure that are used to arrive at the right decision. In some instances they may specify the right choice and conduct, i.e. serve as rules of conduct. More often they hold up that against which various choices and acts are to be measured, i.e. serve as standards of evaluation. Here they serve as a basis of comparison in judging whether or not contemplated actions "measure up." Some decisional and action possibilities are eliminated in light of the norms used, others are affirmed—this is their function of discrimination.

There is a wide variety of norms. Ideals, such as conceptions of love or of justice, function as norms. Goals—attaining personal happiness or raising the level of material well-being, for example—may also work upon decisions and actions in a "norming" fashion. Likewise, models or paradigms are employed—Jesus has often been viewed in Christian ethics as a norm of this kind.

Principles and rules are also used as normative measures. While these two terms are often used interchangeably, it might be helpful to distinguish between them. Basic moral rules usually provide specific determinations for right, wrong and allowed behavior. They convey a community's mind about definite required, forbidden or permitted acts. The Ten Commandments is perhaps the best-known set of such rules in Christian ethics. Principles are usually less specific with respect to conduct and instead provide only general guidance for conduct, or provide direction for the manner in which choices are to be made. "Do unto others as you would have them do unto you." "Why don't you do what others would do in the same circumstances?" "Treat others never as means only, but as ends in themselves." "Never discriminate on the basis of race, sex, creed or national origin."

Norms, as varied in form as ideals, goals, models, principles, and rules, contrast in other ways as well. Some may be general (a conception of love or justice, for example) while others are specific (prohibitions against lying, stealing, and killing). Some carry for some people strict prescriptive authority, while for others the same norms may only be "suggestive" and "illuminative" for decision-making, or "helpful" as a summary of past human experience and reflection. Some norms refer to desirable traits of character, others to desirable actions, still others to both simultaneously. ("Love your neighbor as yourself" has often been understood to refer to both character and conduct.) Some norms refer to the way in which decision-making is to proceed (principles of coherency and consistency are advocated, for example), while others refer to the content of the decision and action itself (the prohibitions against lying, stealing, and killing, to cite examples just mentioned).

Any full treatment of Christian ethics would need to distinguish and discuss norms even further. Our present limited concern can draw the line here, however, and simply reiterate the salient point: decision-making always includes the invoking of various standards of various kinds in order to sort choices and actions. That they are more often assumed than stated or called upon in a conscious manner in no way diminishes their presence and power.

3. The character of the decision-maker will enter into the

choices and actions in many ways, as we have already indicated. Here it is added that something like the following qualification often occurs. Even if *on all other grounds* a particular course of action is judged morally permissible and is recommended, taking it may yet be so out of character with the decision-maker that it is, for that reason, rejected. Another path, more in character, will be chosen. Thus who we are, and what is in keeping with our integrity—these are considerations that frequently come to the fore in choosing and doing.

Each of the three items above, as well as the elements within them, is a separate influence in decision-making and action. A change of one while the others remain the same often means a different stand on the given moral issue. Thus two people holding the same norms and way of deciding, as well as sharing a similar moral character, will often arrive at quite contrasting judgments if they have different understandings of what is occurring and what its meaning is. The same dynamics are true for each of the other variables listed. Two people sharing a similar analysis of the situation may take different stands because they do not share a common character or a similar set of norms. And so on.

Even this cursory overview makes it clear that decision-making has its own set of considerations for Christian ethics. These cannot be subsumed under "the ethics of being" (character) any more than the ethics of being can be regarded as but a facet of "the ethics of doing." Both of these point to major realities in the moral life, intimately related but distinctive. Any effort at comprehensiveness in Christian ethics must come to terms with both.

We pause a final time to ask what concerns critical and normative ethics bring to the subject of decision-making.

Critical ethics will want to know what rules and principles, what ideals, goals and models are appealed to for guidance in answering the question of what it is we ought to do. Critical ethics will also want to hold these up for appraisal. Normative ethics will want to recommend and support a particular way of deciding, a particular set of rules, principles, ideals, goals and models. Christian ethics will, as in the case of the other two areas of persistent concern in ethics, also be engaged in these critical and normative tasks, disclosing, assessing and commending by its own best lights.

In summary, this chapter thus far has attempted to contribute its part towards comprehensiveness for a methodology relating the Bible and ethics by supplying an understanding of the range of concerns and the tasks of Christian ethics as ethics. We have profiled some of the prime realities in the moral life, underlining at the same time the essential unity of the self, the faith it holds, and its decisions and actions. We have located the basic tasks of ethics as disclosure and appraisal of the moral life and commendation of content and means for the living of it. And we have lifted up three areas of continuing concern for ethics, areas which the moral life itself presses to the fore: the location and nature of the good, the nature and character of the moral self, and the factors involved in making choices and undertaking actions.

We have indicated as well that Christian ethics will speak with its own voice on these matters because it has its own primary sources and content and streams of experience and thought. Its own say in ethics may or may not overlap that of some other ethic, but it will of necessity have to be in keeping with, or have integrity with, that which is regarded as central to Christian faith itself. Here it is already clear why the Bible, as the primal record of the formative events and interpretations, is the charter document of the Christian moral life and thus the single most important source for Christian ethics.

Dynamics in the Moral Life

If the foregoing supplies something of the range of concern and the tasks of Christian ethics, it leaves unspecified certain crucial dynamics in the moral life.

1. *The Lines of Influence.* Thus far we have portrayed a certain direction of influences in the moral life, from the self's faith to its acts. This sketch can be misleading. The dynamics of the moral life are such that very strong influences run the other way as well. Being not only shapes doing; doing shapes being. As Aristotle wrote in the *Nicomachean Ethics:* "We become just by doing just acts, temperate by doing temperate acts, brave by doing brave acts." [8] While character informs actions, *acts form character* as well. While our dispositions and intentions shape our judgments and deeds, our judgments and deeds reinforce certain dispositions and intentions and alter others. While the faith we hold and our moral orientation toward things are powerful forces for our responses in a given setting, likewise our responses to specific issues have their formative influences upon how we see life and think about it. The particular forms the general, as well as the general the particular. Indeed, a particularly profound experience in the moral life can recast a great deal of our faith itself, can "convert" us and alter the very consciousness that exercises such power over our choices and acts. More than one person has looked at life differently as a result of some dramatic confrontation with shaking moral choices—the taking of life in war or revolution, for example, or the decision to divest oneself of one's possessions for a very different way of daily living.

Or, to enlarge the picture of the lines of influence, while the faith of the self and its moral meaning are heavily circumscribed and deeply influenced by the particular faiths and moralities of the self's social world, that world's own belief content and conduct may be altered, even substantially, by the self's unique renderings.

The lines of causation in the moral life thus run many ways. Our contention that there is an essential unity of the self and its decisions must be understood in such a way that Christian ethics can legitimately approach it from many angles, from those considerations that belong to the faith and character of the self or from those that belong to its decisions and actions. To choose only one base or one line of influence is methodologically erroneous. (This is reflected, to cite a recurrent example, in the either/or approach posed by those who, on the one hand, say that "ethics' real concern is with hearts and minds" and those who, on the other, say, "no, it's real concern is with the structures of society and the consequences of actions, whatever the motivation and purpose.")

2. *The Communal Dimension.* Several different, although related, notes need to be recorded in view of our *social* nature as human beings.

a) The "seeing" so critical to the moral life is not something we can provide for ourselves by ourselves. It is almost wholly dependent upon relationships with "significant others," whether friend or foe, persons near or far, even real or imaginary. "Seeing" is, in the end, a *community* achievement and gift, whatever the indispensable role of the "I" in attaining sight. For Christian ethics this means at least two things. For its task as critical ethics it means that the nature and life of the self's significant communities is a prime moral reality to be described and assessed. The ethos there will explain much of the participants' ethics. The *corporate* identity or character of these communities will explain much (not all) of the individual identity or character of the members.[9] For the normative task of ethics the community dimensions of perception means that the church as a primary community for the nurturing of moral vision, for helping achieve the gift of sight, is of special importance to the form and content of Christian morality. Christian ethics is indeed *koinonia* ethics. This has been too little explored in Christian ethics. That is a matter of great remiss and strangely out of keeping with the accepted understanding of moral perception as formed and maintained in community.

b) The deeply social nature of our "being," the continual interplay of self and environment that makes us who we are, means there are large-scale social realities and small-scale social realities, as there are relationships of intimacy and intensity and relationships of geographical and psychological distance. There are degrees of privacy in the moral life and degrees of public engagement. The implication is that Christian ethics must include within its range of chief concerns the social systems and structures and institutional patterns of the communities that shape character and conduct. Any assumption that the morality of persons can be understood and dealt with apart from its institutional determinants and institutional expression has missed the particular nature of human "being" as irreducibly social and relational.

c) Those who have chosen to see the structure of the Christian moral life on the terms of a model of relationality and responsibility are right, and on two counts. Empirically, that model is most accurate. That is, human reality itself is at root relational in character, at least those dimensions that have most to do with the moral life. Our morality is essentially a set of responses best understood in view of the reigning relationships. Theologically, the claim for relational or response ethics is also sound. It rests on the assumption that the primary reality in Christian faith is the living God with whom we are in ongoing relationship in community, in a history that is open and for which we share responsibility. The Christian moral life, then, is relational and "responsive" at root because Christian faith itself is a matter of response to this God active in this history.

With this discussion of the directions of influence in the moral life and its communal dimensions, we have added to the earlier presentation. There remains one vital matter to be commented on, however—the uses of the Bible at the critical points in the Christian moral life.

The Uses of the Bible in Christian Ethics

We no longer ask, as in an earlier chapter, about the *actual* uses of the Bible in current Christian ethics. The project at hand is that of proposing the elements of a methodology, so we now ask how *can and ought* the Bible be used in Christian ethics. Answering that question will touch several bases: the kinds of uses of scripture, the kinds of materials used, the starting place for, and the range of, various uses. The general scheme for discussion will follow from the categories outlined above. Thus we shall address essentially two subjects, the Bible and character formation and the Bible and decision-making.

1. *The Bible and Character Formation.* Our contention is that the most effective and crucial impact of the Bible in Christian ethics is that of shaping the moral identity of the Christian and of the church. Until recently this has been discussed only sparingly in Christian ethics. The treatment of those biblical stories, symbols, images, paradigms, and beliefs expressly at the point of their shaping of moral character has found little systematic re-

flection. Indeed, Christian ethics in America has given too little attention to these forms of communication in general, an omission no doubt due to its preoccupation with decision-making and action on specific moral issues. The omission becomes a major one in light of the fact that despite the importance of explicit moral instruction in the moral life, rules, principles, and maxims are surely far less influential than dominating images and symbols, paradigmatic figures, rituals and stories. In all likelihood only a very small part of moral identity and conduct, Christian or otherwise, is the outcome of *explicitly* ethical discourse, even that well internalized in the form of moral instruction. A considerably larger part is the outcome of other forms of communication, much of which on the face of it has no obvious moral point at all.

What about the place of biblical materials in character formation? What might be said, even in exploratory fashion? At what points might these materials shape the kind of person the decision-maker is?

We begin with an illustration. It is perhaps too grand for the limited space available since it is that of the central paradigmatic figure in the Christian moral life. We cannot, of course, replay the New Testament accounts of Jesus' life, death, and resurrection. But we can imagine for illustrative purposes that a certain person has found in Jesus the object of her final loyalty, devotion and commitment and seeks to take from him the clues for her own way of being and doing. We can then ask what this implies regarding the role of the Bible.

She has a certain portrait of Jesus she regards as authentic. In that portrait Jesus identifies with the outcasts in society and trusts in God as Father, with apparently little or no anxiety about his own needs or his place and power in society. He also portrays compassion, a humble service, a willingness to endure unmerited suffering and face certain tragedy resolutely, a gentleness toward nature and a harshness about human arrogance.

We do not ask whether this person's portrait of Jesus is accurate. Rather we speculate about this: assuming such a portrait has become in fact a paradigm of Christian conduct for this person, at what points will it matter for morality? Putting aside the impact of other influences, biblical or non-biblical, her *perception, dispositions,* and *intentions* might be affected along something like the following lines.

Her general way of seeing life might become characterized by a set of acquired and nurtured moral sensitivities that search out those often invisible to many in society—the poor, the outcast, the ill, and infirm. She might come to possess a basic posture toward life that is more sensitive than most to human suffering and is at the same time unconcerned with her own needs. She might have a "feel" for where people hurt and be able to empathize deeply. She might acquire certain specific dispositions, such as an attitude of initial strong trust in people and a lack of suspicion and fear of strangers, an underlying hopefulness about improvement of the human lot, a deep appreciation for non-human life in the world of nature, and a severe impatience with people's claims to high and enduring achievement. There may be particular intentions present as well, all of them with plausible ties to the reigning example of Jesus in her life: to always seek non-violent resolution to conflict; to champion the causes of the oppressed; to seek the kingdom of God before all else.

What painted this compelling, exemplary figure for her? A collage of biblical materials. Perhaps the healing and feeding narratives; the parable of the Good Samaritan and the cycle of the lost sheep, coin, and son; the teachings on the mountain; Jesus' announcement of his ministry in Luke 4; and the events of Passion Week. Probably others as well. We list these few simply to register the possibility that a set of biblical materials has portrayed a paradigmatic figure who became for this person a chief source for her way of looking at the world and responding to it. The content of the paradigm helped "define what was real" for her; it generated a certain set of moral priorities rather than some other; and it disposed her to act and react in patterns that set her on one course instead of another. Her motives, attitudes, values, and intentions flowed from what she felt and hoped was in keeping with her model of the genuinely good life, that of Jesus.

Our choice of influential biblical materials might have been different and could, in any case, be extended almost indefinitely. We have chosen only one, that of an exemplary figure portrayed by scripture. (The particular one chosen has a special place, to be sure.) The contention is simply that the Bible can and ought to be a major force in molding perspectives, dispositions, and intentions.

It might be helpful to select an example less grand. For instance, how might a pictorial presentation from one of the parables affect character formation? The image of the Good Samaritan, if internalized as a major image, might evoke a general perspective that sees all humankind as a single family under God, and it might evoke the specific intention of helping to break down the barriers that in fact still separate "Jew" and "Samaritan," male and female, bond and free. Some particular dispositions might be engendered by this image: a readiness to respond to human need as such, whether that of perceived friend or perceived foe, or a consistent inclination to move toward rather than away from the stranger. Particular convictions might be elicited as well: keeping faith with God is aiding the neighbor; attending to human need is a compelling Christian duty; the gospel means banishing enmity and hostility.

Again the point is not *which* biblical materials generate *which* perspectives, attitudes, intentions and convictions, but *that* biblical materials *can and ought* to create a cast which has profound ramifications for character and conduct. Certain choices and actions would be eliminated from the outset, others affirmed, and a few never appear on the horizon as possibilities at all. In other words, if character is the chief architect of our conduct, *Christian* character might have its own major materials in the biblical resources.

We have no desire to oversimplify. We are aware both that many sources other than biblical ones have great influence on Christian moral identity and that among the biblical sources themselves there is great variety (this includes morally conflicting materials). A singular presentation of the Bible's meaning for Christian character is not possible, nor is a singular presentation of normative Christian character. We wish only to suggest that the role of the scriptures in the nurturing of a basic orientation and in the generating of particular attitudes and intentions is a central one.

The question arises, which materials are to be used? It is not evasive to say that for character formation the whole panorama of biblical materials is in view, from symbols and narratives to theological ruminations and devotional elements. The shaping of Christian identity engages them all in some way or another, at different moments in different settings for different purposes. Yet it is extremely difficult to say with any precision just which materials can and ought to be used for which times, places and purposes. Why?

The reason resides in the nature of moral development and the multi-faceted character of many biblical materials. Moral identity cannot at base be separated from the person's identity in general. It is a *dimension* of that identity rather than some self-contained piece of it. This gestalt nature of identity prohibits any easy directing of biblical materials (or any other) specifically and exclusively along lines of moral development.

The drama of the Eucharist can be cited for illustrative purposes. Is participation in this drama a devotional, aesthetic, or moral experience shaping the way we look at life? It may be experienced as any or all of these. At a given time its overt *moral* impact, affecting our sensibilities concerning good and evil, may be considerable or negligible for us as worshipers. At the very same time its *devotional* impact may be an indelible one, surrounding us with a sense of the sacred. Yet the nature of identity formation is such that the devotional impact may itself have an indirect influence upon moral development. The sense of the sacred might nourish attitudes of awe and wonder that become part of our moral profile. In the end, then, biblical materials may enter the process of character formation in ways very difficult to trace.

What can be said with certainty about these materials and the formation of character is that Christian ethics needs to guard against every form of what might be called "genre reductionism." This is the effective selection, whether deliberate or not, of only certain kinds of biblical materials as the materials pertinent to ethics. Thus the wisdom sayings, moral teachings and prophetic injunctions are used, and the devotional materials, apocalyptic visions and miracle stories are not. The nature of character formation itself belies such apparently "obvious" distinctions for Christian ethics.

The nature of formation is not the only reason to avoid genre reductionism, however. A primary part of what it has meant historically to be a Christian is to place oneself into interaction with the *whole* scripture and its influence. To fractionize and reduce the canon has always been regarded as a *theological* heresy. For the sake of Christian *ethics,* it is to be resisted as well.

Of course the different materials may work in different ways. The theological discourses, those of Paul or the author of Job, for example, might be the source of certain reasoned convictions and beliefs of the faith. These then have their influence upon character in their own mode: what the person regards as propositional truth shapes who he or she is. The apocalyptic visions might be stimuli to a broader vision that in turn alters, even if ever so slightly, the way we see the world—some things come alive with meanings we did not discern before those strange images illumined them for us. The piety of the devotional materials might impress within us certain attitudes of mystery, humility, dependence and reverence that carry over into our moral habits. The nature psalms, for example, might move us toward a different response to the environment. The miracle stories, (the feeding of the five thousand, for example) might on one level of meaning carry over as the reinforcing of certain intentions (the resolution to feed the hungry in Jesus' name). At no point can we say on principle which biblical materials belong to those affecting the development of moral character, and which do not. Thus Christian ethics, while it must seek to decipher what in fact the effects of different kinds of materials are, must not succumb to genre reductionism.

Another question arises. Where is the starting point for Christian ethics in its use of the Bible for character formation? Again it is not evasion if we say, "Almost anywhere, but usually not with the decision or issue at hand." The use of the Bible in the development of moral character is a matter of long-term nurture. Thus the attention of Christian ethics here is not to a currently provoking moral issue but to the ongoing worship and educational life of the church above all, and to the extensions and expressions of these in the family. This is another area of relative neglect in American Christian ethics and we will discuss it in the ensuing chapter. For now the concern is to underline the moral importance of a continual immersion in biblical materials in worship and education. In a word, the starting point for moral identity is with the Bible in the life of the church as a gathered community.

It might be helpful to draw attention at this juncture to a distinction between the use of the *Bible* in Christian ethics and the use of *biblical scholarship*. Or, more precisely, between the use of the Bible with a heavy dependence on biblical scholarship around particular texts and a use far less dependent on the findings of current scholarship. The use of the Bible throughout most of the liturgy would be an example of the latter. Its use in homiletical materials in the liturgy would be an example of the former, however.

The reason for drawing attention to such a distinction here is that, by and large, the use of the Bible in the formation of character, through the recital of images, stories, historical narratives, rituals, and paradigms in the educational and worship life of the church, may not always draw on the world of biblical scholarship (in liturgical life, for example). Even when biblical scholarship *is* drawn upon for uses of the Bible directed to nurturing identity, through such as educational programs, the scholarship employed is not necessarily focused on Christian ethics directly. The situation is different, however, when Christian ethics turns to the use of the Bible for decision-making and action on particular moral issues. Here the attention to specific texts in order to come to terms with specific moral issues will entail much more of the indispensible critical work that biblical scholarship offers. Hence the dependence of Christian ethics on biblical studies is a more direct one and its use of the Bible more closely tied to the work of biblical scholars. We must turn now to this topic of decision-making.

2. *The Bible and Decision-Making.* While the place of the Bible in decision-making and action on moral issues does not, in our judgment, match in significance its potential influence in character formation, there are nonetheless several important points of contact. The Bible's directness and degree of influence varies considerably among them, as we shall note.

The elements that consistently come to the fore in ethical decisions, outlined earlier in the chapter, will serve as our framework.

a) The person's (or group's) analysis of the decision-situation and the understanding of the critical data and issues thrusts us immediately into a dual set of judgments about the place of scriptures. At certain points the biblical influence is negligible or non-existent. A thorough analysis of a moral issue and its setting will entail the use of certain data-gathering and analytical skills that are technical in nature and which have no significant relationship to any biblical materials at all. Many of the tools provided by the social sciences, life sciences, and natural sciences are of this kind and they play an indispensable role in Christian ethics. But even in the less formal analysis of many of our day-to-day decisions we employ a wide range of organizing and appraising skills we have learned as part of the culture's folk knowledge, skills with no perceptible connection to biblical materials. Here the Bible is of little import even though the task at hand is a critical one.

At other points, however, the impact of the Bible upon understanding and analysis may be considerable. What we regard as the significant data (necessarily a value judgment) and the overriding moral issues in any given set of circumstances will reflect our perception of things, our angle of vision. Thus even basic apprehension is directly connected to that complex marriage of faith, character, and perception. In this way the internalizing of biblical materials in ways formative of our outlook may have its real, though indirect, impact.

The person mentioned in our earlier example can be brought to mind again. Her internalizing of that portrait of Jesus would sort the data and issues for her in a way that might yield a different analysis from that of someone living life by a contrasting paradigm.

b) The norms or standards brought to bear in decision-making may well show considerable influence from biblical materials. This influence may be *indirect* yet significant, as when the Bible has shaped widely held cultural norms. In this case those who may not grant the Bible any authority in their lives, indeed may openly reject it as an informing source for conduct, may yet employ moral norms that have, *via* a long history, some biblical roots. A certain notion of justice, a high regard for human life, a press toward equality, or basic moral rules in the form of civil law would be examples in many settings.

A more *direct* influence upon moral norms can take a variety of forms. The Bible might be regarded, as it has often been, as the source of a revealed norm of its own. Agapeic love is an example central in much of American Christian ethics in this century. The biblical notion of "shalom" has yet to be fully explored as another norm. The understanding of "righteousness" so rich throughout the Old Testament is a closely related one.

The biblical materials might directly supply norms in a somewhat different manner. The Bible might be, as it has often been, the major source of theological categories which encompass many moral norms. The terms of the theological framework become the terms for decision-making as these are worked out exegetically. Karl Barth, to cite one prominent example, first establishes exegetically the grand theological themes of creation and covenant. Then he uses these norm-laden themes for discussing several matters fraught with moral issues and choices—marriage and child-bearing, the functions of the state, economic life, abortion, euthanasia, capital punishment.[10] Here, and Barth is but one of many possible examples, biblical norms enter decision-making by way of theological motifs on the basis of which specific moral choices are rendered. The norms used are scriptural in origin and thus the Bible's influence remains direct.

Sometimes the biblical materials work differently, however. Rather than supplying a distinctive, revealed norm of their own, or a cluster of them, they work so as to transform the norms already common to the human enterprise. Thus an Augustine or an Aquinas was not simply accommodating or being hypocritical in affirming certain pagan norms and asserting their ethical integrity even while these norms needed transformation in light of biblical revelation. The norms, then, might originate in many quarters of the human experience. The biblical materials rank, illumine, and transform them.

Our contention is that the Bible can and ought to be a source of moral norms for the Christian life. At the same time, and for almost any given decision, it will not function as the sole source of norms. Nor should it. But that anticipates a discussion we take up later—the Bible's authority in Christian ethics and the relation of biblical to non-biblical materials.

The role of biblically influenced norms will be a double one. Negatively, some otherwise plausible norms will be ruled out. Positively, a different set will be confirmed or "authorized." An example of the former is ethical egoism. A case can be made for this. An individual's single basic obligation is to promote his or her own welfare as he or she defines that. Individual well-being, self-defined, when cast as *the* moral standard runs strongly counter to the biblical grain, however. There *whatever* norm is considered must, at its base, be more other-regarding and self-denying than ethical egoism. Here, then, is a norm ruled out by the overwhelming testimony of the scriptures, even when a strong philosophical case might be made for it on other grounds. An example of a norm positively confirmed by the canon would be distributive justice, obliging people of similar abilities to make the same relative contributions and sacrifices in the communities they inhabit. Such a norm can summon biblical support that is not simply proof-texting or contorted theologizing from "well-chosen" materials. It would rally support from throughout the canon.

Thus, whether or not the biblical materials actually supply some of the norms for Christian ethics (and we assume they can and ought to), they influence the boundaries for all proposed norms from whatever sources. Some will be considered in bounds for Christian ethics, others out of bounds. Precisely which of the large number of remaining possibilities is most "faithful" for the Christian moral life is the subject of continuing debate in Christian ethics and in biblical studies. We cannot engage in that debate within the space available here. But we do need to parallel what was said about genre with the same for moral norms. It is methodologically erroneous to proceed with the assumption of a single biblical norm for Christian ethics. "Norm-reductionism" is to be combatted as vigorously as genre reductionism. This of course is not grounds for an utter norm relativism. Nor is it grounds for an indiscriminate pluralism. Any full discussion must face those tough questions about which norms should be the reigning ones in Christian ethics.

Do the biblical materials supply normative rules and principles for Christian ethics? Are there biblically rooted or influenced imperatives with the force of moral law? Our contention is, yes, there are. That affirmation doesn't answer a number of critical questions, however. How is the specific content determined? What would be the present fulfillment or "application" of the biblically grounded command? Are exceptions morally possible, and, if so, on what grounds? Are there biblical grounds for abrogating moral law as such under some circumstances? Without launching a discussion that would require a further volume, we can say some things which designate the way in which the Bible can properly be a source of moral rules and principles as norms in Christian ethics.

Any proposed rule or principle would need consistent backing throughout that corpus which defines the identity of the Christian and the church. In other words, a prescription of behavior that claimed to express authentic Christian identity would need to be able to demonstrate canonical integrity. The injunctions toward the poor, discussed in a later chapter, are examples of imperatives with such backing.

The biblical materials might not only provide straight-forward prescriptions, however. They might also be the source of guidelines *for locating the burden of proof* on a given moral issue and choice.

War and revolution, for example, or even a case of assault on a normally peaceful neighborhood street, can force that moral turbulence which questions whether or not there is a justifiable taking of human life. In the heat of battle that question will be answered one way or another, with little or no reflection. But in a previous time of relative calm, or a later one, the person may ask for aid in making up his or her mind. The biblical materials can help locate the burden of proof. In this case, the scriptures mandate that the general rule be one against the taking of life.

If there is any exception to be made that has moral integrity, then it must be one which at least begins with a non-violent bearing as the normal and normative one for the Christian. That is, the use of lethal violence is *not on the same level of choice* with non-violence, or even non-lethal violence. Its use, if allowed at all, requires a special justification. Further, that special justification itself would also need biblical warrants. Thus just war teachings in Christian ethics have sought scriptural grounds for an exceptional but morally permissible use of deadly violence. The point is that the biblical materials can function as the source of normative rules of rather specific content in Christian ethics—rules which set the terms for locating the burden of proof.

A closely related use is that of setting limits for morally permitted conduct, i.e., rules and principles that mark the edges, declaring what is out of bounds. The "shalt not's" of the Ten Commandments have functioned this way.

Rules and principles in Christian ethics may, then, be influenced by biblical materials in several ways:

• as the source for positive prescription in keeping with the basic identity of the Christian as Christian;

• as the source for establishing the boundaries of morally permissible behavior;

• as the source for locating where the burden of proof lies, or what the normal and normative bearing will be, and what kind of case constitutes a morally justified exception.

It should be added that the rules, principles, and other norms in Christian ethics may show considerable influence from biblical sources even when they are not *directly* taken from them. Indeed, norms often need to be "created." This is frequently the case when Christians face novel issues. Current biomedical technology has presented many such issues. A search for guidelines for fetal research is but one example. For the creation of new norms the course usually taken is to work from broader principles with biblical warrants, such as notions of the sanctity and the quality of life.

c) Any thorough treatment of the method of practical moral reasoning (or the steps for approaching and moving through a decision on a moral matter) entails more considerations than we can entertain here. In view of our major concerns several helpful statements can be made, however.

It is significant for Christian ethics that no single biblical way of making decisions exists. The scriptures give evidence of several modes. Thus an appeal by Christian ethics to the sources would not of itself settle the issue of the method to be preferred, even if the Bible were granted such authority in decision-making. Brevard Childs' observation, cited earlier, is worth noting again:

> It is of fundamental importance to recognize that at no point within the Bible is there ever spelled out a system or a technique by which one could move from the general imperatives of the law of God, such as found in the Decalogue, to the specific application within the concrete situation.[11]

At the same time, certain characteristics persist in the biblical materials in which decision-making is portrayed. These can be appropriated by Christian ethics as clues for its own determinations.

(1) The diversity in the Bible might itself suggest that singularity of method ought not be a matter of obsession in Christian ethics. The suggestion is that different decision-situations might legitimately be handled with different responses.[12] The applica-

tion of agreed-upon principles through a form of casuistry might work very well in one instance, while a contextualist approach for highly contingent and unusual factors might better serve in another. Without further work this suggestion would beg the methodological question of determining which method is most appropriate when, and how one method might relate to another in an encompassing theory. But at least the biblical pluralism ought to give pause and stave off the methodological reductionism that can so easily characterizes Christian ethics.

(2) A biblically influenced method would have as one mark the community setting and community experience. Decision-making is overwhelmingly a community enterprise in the biblical materials. Whatever method or methods Christian ethics might choose as its own, the church would function as a major community of moral deliberation.

(3) In the biblical materials making decisions and taking stands appears to happen between two poles, that of a responsible sense of obligation to the community's standards and traditions on the one hand, and a creative or innovating freedom on the other. The burden of deciding and acting is never removed and the decision is always taken in freedom. Yet, it is never a rootless freedom or one without accountability to community precedent, experience and norms. A way of approaching and moving to and through a decision in Christian ethics would take account of these poles, again if the biblical materials are used as clues.

(4) Whatever the particular method, it would need to be in keeping with Christian ethics as at root relational or response ethics. The touchstone for Israel's morality and that of the early church is always the faith-experience of God. All the elements

used in determining which behavior is most fitting in a given set of circumstances take their form and function from this faith relationship. This means, to cite but one example, that rules, principles and other norms in the decision-making process are viewed as expressive of underlying relationships, indicating their kind, quality, and content. The rules, principles and other norms take their authority from the defining relationships, not the reverse. The Ten Commandments are never viewed or understood by Israel apart from the relationship-defining "preamble" that introduces them: "I am the Lord your God who brought you out of Egypt, out of the house of bondage." The biblical materials themselves indicate that whatever method of moral reasoning is used in Christian ethics, it needs to be in keeping with relational or response ethics. It needs to be a method that continually refers the decision-maker to the animating core of Christian morality in the living relationship with God.

d) We must turn now to questions of the kind of biblical materials used in decision-making and the proper starting point for their use.

The decision-situation and the provoking moral issue set the agenda for the conversation between the Bible and Christian ethics. One starts from the issue and its matrix and goes from there to the biblical materials, quite in contrast to the flow in character formation.

The starting point directly affects the biblical materials used. Whatever their genre, they will be sought because they address the particular issue at hand and/or illumine the situation. Thus a case engaging the moral issue of civil obedience and disobedience might turn to portions of scripture such as the admonitions of Peter and Paul to be subordinate to the ordained powers, or to the portrayal of the state as the beast in Revelation 13.

Certain events in the life of Jesus might be consulted, such as those involving his relationship with the Zealots. These uncover a wrestling with the relevant issues of acquiring of political power and employing violence as a means. Note that even in this brief example several different forms of biblical literature are cited—moral admonition, apocalyptic vision, and historical account. But in contrast with the more generalized use of the Bible for character formation, here all are appropriated for a single, sharp focus upon a specific moral issue. Here, too, as mentioned earlier, the detailed work of biblical scholars on particular texts will be essential.

The focus on the particular does not mean, however, that only those materials *directly* addressing the issue are usable, or even the most important. For decision-making, as for moral development, there are virtually limitless possibilities in the rich symbols, accounts, images, and exemplary figures. There may be no clear and straightforward moral point in their textual presentation. Yet they may in one setting or another function as a source of decisive insight for the matter at hand. The symbols of bread and wine capture for some Christians a deep caring for the earth (among other meanings). The Eucharist generates and expresses for them a Christ-centered nature mysticism. In the face of actions oblivious to environmental welfare, these symbols illumine for these Christians the general direction of their action, even when no one particular policy is indicated. Or the Old Testament account of the Jubilee Year might for some enter into their dreams and choices for economic and political life, even when it does not do so by way of an "application" or "translation." It functions as a mind-expanding picture, a stimulus to creative vision.

Here we begin to wander into vaguely charted territory. It is the realm of the imagination in decision-making and the role of the Bible in provoking the imagination of the person in search of insight.

Imagination clearly plays a major role in making up our minds. Most of our decisions are not made by passing through tight syllogisms that have their top line in some general moral principle. Rather, an image or model or way of proceeding is brought from some other setting, often from some apparently unrelated body of knowledge, and is used "imaginatively" as illumination for what might be done.

The link with biblical materials is a vital one. They may serve as the source for the materials of imagination. Indeed, a too-easy insistence upon *directly* addressing specific moral issues often truncates severely what the Bible has to offer for decision-making. Often the best offered is precisely that which has no pertinence to the exigencies of the moment, *as we define them*. Instead, through those seemingly strange stories and images, allegories and parables, entered into by imagination, a different place to stand or a different angle of vision is acquired, a different world is inhabited. Often that is exactly what is needed. From there a constellation of resources may also be available, many of which may not be at hand in the decision-maker's own immediate cultural context. That, too, is often exactly what is needed.

What we are pointing to is exemplified by William Stringfellow's book, *An Ethic for Christians and Other Aliens in a Strange Land*. There a critique of America is played out between the 137th Psalm ("By the waters of Babylon . . ."), the Book of Revelation, and Stringfellow's understanding of the last quarter century of American life. Stringfellow throughout links ancient imagery and present reality and uses scripture as the source of a different, informing perspective. His task, as he says,

. . . is to treat the nation within the tradition of biblical politics—to understand America biblically—*not* the other way around, *not* (to put it in an appropriately awkward way) to construe the Bible Americanly.[13]

With this note on the Bible and imagination we have come full circle. The discussion has been that of the Bible's role in decision-making. But the nurturing of imagination so critical to decision-making turns out also to be of a piece with the formation of character. It is formative of both seeing and deciding. The starting point or occasion may be different—addressing the moral issue at hand in the one instance, participating in the ongoing life of the church as a worshiping, learning community in the other. Yet the different starting points represent only different points on the lines of influence. Seeing shapes decisions and actions. Decisions and actions form and alter perception. And in both, the same diverse biblical materials are used "imaginatively" to work the double influence. The uses of the Bible in identity formation and the uses of the Bible in decision-making play upon one another in a mutually animating way.[14]

The role of the church in the Christian's seeing and deciding, and in relating Bible and ethics to these, has been hinted at often in these pages. The task now is to explore that more fully as a crucial component of our methodology.

4 the church as community context

What we are able to discern and do in the moral life results from our participation in various communities. What has been done to us and for us in our social world sets most of the terms for our general bearing in life and even for our specific responses to particular moral issues. "Seeing," as we said in the previous chapter, is a community achievement and gift, something we cannot provide for ourselves by ourselves. Nor is decision-making a self-enclosed undertaking, however deeply personal and sometimes lonely some choices may be. The very materials of even the most private decisions are acquired by the self in its social experience. *Homo ethicus* is *homo socius*.

It would be curious in the extreme, then, if we discussed the Christian moral life without discussing the Christian community, if we did not make extensive reference to that community charged above all with the forming and reforming of Christian character and conduct. It would be even more curious if we discussed the relation of the Bible and Christian ethics at book-length without extensive reference to the only community for whom the Old and New Testament are the scriptures and the only community charged with the functional relating of these scriptures to life. Yet a treatment of the church as the necessary and decisive community context for Christian ethics, including the appropriation of biblical materials, has been largely neglected in American Christian ethics, especially Protestant ethics.[1]

Drawing out the reasons for this neglect need not occupy us here, although undoubtedly one of them is the preoccupation with decision-making and action we mentioned earlier. When the church has come into view at all, this preoccupation has pressed only certain limited questions to the fore: "who speaks for the church and how does the church speak on moral matters?" Those questions have generated extensive debate at local, denominational, and ecumenical levels. Yet they have failed to ask whether in some broader and more foundational sense the church is the necessary and decisive community for the full range of Christian ethical concerns, including the appropriation of the Bible for the moral life.

A wider net must be cast. Just as the preoccupation with decision-making and action has often constricted the very understanding of what comprises Christian ethics, so the focus on the church's *speaking on* moral *issues* has truncated the understanding of the church in Christian ethics, not least at the point of relating Bible and ethics. Thus if the following pages fail to focus on those questions about how and through whom the church speaks, it is not because they are unimportant. Any full treatment of Christian ethics must engage them extensively. Rather, it is because they encompass too little.

The intent of this chapter, to outline a more central role for the church than it has generally been given in American Christian ethics, rests upon certain assumptions about the relationship of scripture and church in the moral life. These assumptions go to the heart of this book and we will consider them in the course of the following discussion.

We suggest three ways in which the church can and ought to function as the chief community context for Christian ethics. These ways are closely related yet sufficiently distinct from one another to merit separate comment: the church as a shaper of Christian moral identity; the church as a bearer of moral tradition; and the church as a community of moral deliberation. For each function three facets will be discussed: the meaning of the function in a general way for the moral life; the relationship of the church to the function discussed; and the place of the scriptures for that function in the church.

The Church as a Shaper of Moral Identity

The place of human communities in forming and reforming moral character has been underscored frequently in these pages. Thus we can turn directly to the church as one of those communities of identity formation and ask about its place in Christian ethics.

It is instructive to note the character of Christian ethics in its origins. For the early church, as for Israel, the community of faith was the starting point and the continual reference point for determining fitting conduct. Members did not so much ask, even by implication, "What is the universal good and what action on our part would be in accord with it." They asked, in effect, "What action on our part is in keeping with who we are as the people of God." Doing flowed from being and being was defined by the nature of the community. Everything was referred to the community as the moral nexus. In that setting daily affairs were connected to the shared memory, mission, and destiny. Thus even when non-Christian and non-Jewish sources of ethical wisdom were adopted and pressed into service, as they often were, they were filtered through the self-understanding of the community, asked to meet its norms and standards and to conform to its corporate moral temper. So the *koinonia,* while itself altered by these materials, also gave them its own cast, in keeping with the way life looked from within a vision that took its contours from the life, death, and resurrection of Jesus Christ. In a word, the early church was for its members *the* community context of being and doing.

This is not yet to say how the church can and ought to shape the moral identity of its members. It is only to observe that it functioned as such a community in its origins. Christian ethics was community ethics in a thoroughgoing way; it was *koinonia* ethics.

Before addressing how the church forms and nourishes moral identity, we need to be clear about the relationship of the church and the scriptures.[2] The relationship is a dialectical one.

1. *Apart from the scriptures, the church has no enduring identity as church.* An essential part of what it means to be "the Christian church" is to be the community of the Christian scriptures. Of course, it is God-in-Christ and not the scriptures that constitutes the church's raison d'etre. But since the formation of the canon the scriptures have been the central source of the church's knowledge of those events which called it into being. This has affected in an essential way its doctrine and teaching, its symbols and lore, its liturgy and preaching, its care and mission. The church's self-understanding, its speech, and its action are all inseparable from the use of the Bible as its scriptures. They carry "authority" in and for its common life. Without the scriptures the church would not be the church.

2. *Apart from the church, the scriptures as Christian scriptures*

have no context or voice. The Bible has historical, cultural, and literary interest and value apart from the church; but *as Christian scripture* the Bible has no meaningful setting or ongoing medium outside of the church. Part of what it means to say "the Christian scriptures" is to say they carry formative weight in this community and apart from this community they have no enduring community.

If the scriptures establish and maintain, as a mediating authority, the church's corporate identity as church, what is it they do in and through the common life of the gathered community? *They form and reform personal identities in a decisive (or transforming) way.* Part of what it means to be "church," normatively speaking, is to shape individual lives in keeping with the church's own corporate identity. This is done when the scriptures are used in the community's common life in ways that mediate the presence of God.

The next question becomes, *how* does the church shape identity, moral identity in particular? We can call on earlier discussions and thus be brief. There we noted that just as no principled way exists of sorting biblical materials with any precision along the lines of their moral influence, so no principled way exists of separating moral identity from the person's whole being. Neither is there a way to mark off precisely which elements in the church's common life will affect moral identity in particular.

How, then, does the Bible in the church shape moral character? Or, more accurately, how does the church, with the Bible, do so? We mention essentially two ways, without attempting to specify which aspects work in exactly what manner.

The first is as one of the communities directly formative of perception, dispositions, and intentions. The church can and ought directly to nurture the Christian's "relational capacities." [3] These are character traits such as sensitivity and empathy, security, trust, and courage. They are "pre-ethical" capacities in the sense that they exercise decisive influences on our conduct *prior to* our rational deliberation of specific choices around given issues. Our earlier discussion encompassed them as "dispositions" and we need not point out again their importance and power in our conduct. We do need to point out that they are acquired only in community. The church can and ought to be a community formative of such capacities.

An example is in order. The church might, through worship and education rooted in its scriptures, effectively communicate as part of the faith our unconditional acceptance by God. Whether we live well or not, believe rightly or not, feel at peace or not, live on good terms with our neighbors or not, we are accepted by God and nothing we do or fail to do alters that. Such a communication might in turn have the effect of generating in us a disposition to accept others with less regard to the human standards we had previously imposed. We might have something approaching a basic equal regard for others, whatever their personal attractiveness or the nature of their actions. Or this communication, if internalized, might generate a security that permits us to take risks we might not have taken if God-acceptance and self-acceptance had hinged upon our performance in the moral life, if they had hinged upon the rightness and wrongness of our decisions and deeds.

Here acceptance and security represent specific "relational capacities" the church can and ought to nurture as part of the shaping of character.

Another brief example might be suggestive, this time for the matter of basic outlook. If the liturgical and instructional life of the church again and again presents the biblical symbols of the cross and resurrection as dominating symbols, they might elicit an outlook that sees life laced with deeply tragic and ironic dimensions yet never beyond renewal and redemption, never incapable of new being. The contrast with life symbols that communicated not only tragic and ironic dimensions but also a fully fated destiny would be dramatic for conduct in the moral life. The contrast with symbols that communicated an easy optimism about life and an expectation of full, immediate gratification of personal needs and desires would be equally dramatic.

The list of illustrations must not lose the main point: one way the church can and ought to mold the moral character of its members is through the *direct* formation of elements of character.

There is a second means. It is by ordering the influences on character. Here the church can and ought to be *the integrating community* for the Christian's various loyalties and loves, commitments and convictions, attitudes and intentions, values and goals, as these are brought from many sources, from within the church and without. The church can provide a "centering" for the multiple claims and influences that originate in the Christian's social world. It can, in different words, be the community that orders the faith we live by and sets in place the images, symbols and stories that reign in our lives, whether their source is in the community of faith or outside it. The church thus can shape moral identity by facilitating "integrity" in the primary sense of that word—an integration at the core of our being.

Such an integration would occur in accord with the church's claim, biblically-based, that God in Christ is the center of value, the final object of our most basic loyalty, trust and devotion, the ultimate source of goodness and power. The competing claims for our allegiance and commitment that permeate our everyday world would be adjudicated and assigned their roles in keeping with this overriding conviction that God in Christ is the final authority in the Christian moral life.

As with the more direct forming and nurturing of the elements of character, here, too, the means would include the full range of resources in the life of the gathered community. Liturgy and sacraments, doctrine and teaching, preaching and counseling are some that might be named. Their ties to the Christian scriptures need not be reiterated.

We can summarize the importance of the church and its scriptures as a shaper of moral identity. The Christian has no enduring identity *as Christian* apart from the church. Thus the church is the necessary context for relating the Christian's moral life to his or her identity *as Christian*. This includes relating the biblical materials directly and indirectly. The church and no other community has the task of shaping moral identity through the use of the Christian scriptures. Whatever else it may be, Christian ethics is not Christian ethics without and apart from the church and its scriptures.

The Church as a Bearer of Moral Tradition

The church as a former of identity and the church as a bearer of moral tradition overlap one another, as we shall see. First we ask about the functions of moral tradition in general as the necessary backdrop for discussing the church as the bearer of a specific tradition.

Three functions are sketched in what follows: moral tradition as an aid for moral development; moral tradition as a source of content for an ethic; and moral tradition as a framework of accountability in the moral life. We take each in turn.

For moral development, as for personality development in general, it is axiomatic that we know, or at least deeply sense, who we are in order to become who we are not yet but desire to be. We must be able to locate ourselves before we can go anywhere. And knowing who we are means in part knowing the tradition or traditions in which we are rooted. Our moral growth and maturity thus requires being part of a moral history and being aware of it as a part of us. Lack of such a tradition, or lack of the consciousness of it, results in moral drift, a values-limbo that leaves the person bewildered and incoherent in the moral life.

This is not to imply that any particular moral tradition is to be affirmed in blanket fashion. Much is often morally dubious. Some is occasionally morally outrageous. Again and again nothing is so imperative as simply leaving strains of the tradition behind. (As we write, the issue of the ordination of women is front-page news.) Yet even breaking with one line or another in a given moral tradition—or with whole bodies of it—requires taking it seriously as one's own heritage and as a solid point of reference. It might be added that often the best resource for correcting a tradition lies within the tradition itself, as the ecumenical movement has demonstrated in classic fashion. In the Christian moral life an appeal to some neglected portrait of Jesus has often served in this way, as have numerous other appeals to scripture.

Moral tradition also supplies many of the materials for the fashioning of an ethic by which to live and die. Within it are included diverse interpretations of the faith or faiths, together with their corollary moralities. If the tradition has been an expansive one wide-ranging views on a virtually endless number of moral issues are also included. The embodiments of different life patterns are also part of a tradition, as is a wealth of portraits, symbols, images, stories, rituals, and visions. On a reflective, critical level, the moral tradition usually includes a continual scrutiny of the different claims of the respective faith or faiths for the moral life, as well as a ceaseless debate about the rights and wrongs of particular stands and particular patterns of living.

The variety that makes up a moral tradition, at least a major one, is thus usually very rich. It offers much of the fund from which the person can fashion his or her own ethic. Expressed differently, a moral tradition is a major source for answering the question of "the good" for a person's life, and for following out its meaning in the various arenas of the person's existence.

Thirdly, moral tradition provides a framework of accountability. The self is, by virtue of being a part of a tradition, set within a matrix of moral claims and concerns. It is tied to a community or communities in a common history that shows the self what character and conduct is responsible, as that history understands responsibility. The tradition thus supplies a governing influence in the moral life by mediating the claims of "significant others," past, present and future, claims about who we are to be and what we are to do.

Turning now to the church we ask first about the relationship of the church and the faith tradition of which the Christian moral tradition is part.

As the ecumenical movement has clarified, the church is the locus, as well as the agent, of a tradition. That is, the tradition is both the *activity of handing on* the faith and *that which is handed on.*[4]

Part of the tradition—the single most decisive or "authoritative" part—is the church's scripture. It is not *alongside* tradition, as if we were speaking of two separate but equal (or unequal) authorities. Rather the scriptures are the primary voice within the tradition, so intimately a part that we can say we know no Christian tradition except as formed by the Christian scriptures *and* we know no scriptures as Christian scriptures except as part of Christian tradition. Indeed, a very sizeable portion of Christian tradition is little other than the history of biblical interpretation and the believing community's response to it (in doctrine, liturgy, polity, ethics, and elsewhere).

What do the scriptures as part of tradition, and tradition as "a single complex whole," [5] do in the common life of the church? Tradition nurtures and safeguards the identity of the church as church. Within that corporate identity the personal identities of members are formed as Christians.

But how, specifically, does the church's *moral* tradition, as part of the "single complex whole," function? Here we return to the earlier discussion. If the reader will call to mind the three functions of moral tradition, we can be very brief.

The church is, normatively speaking, a major source and resource for moral development. It is this whenever it sets Christians within a moral tradition with which they can identify.

The church is the rich and varied fund for the content of the Christian's ethic. When it embodies and passes on its moral tradition it supplies such a fund.

The church is the framework of accountability for the Christian moral life. When the church lets its moral tradition form and inform its ongoing life, it functions as this framework.

We conclude this section with an assertion. There is only one community that undertakes to relate Christians' specific moral choices and acts to their identity *as Christians*. That community is the church. The church is a bearer of moral tradition, and the scriptures are the heart of that tradition.

We turn next to the third major function of the church for Christian ethics: the church as a community of moral deliberation. As we shall see, the focus here will be on decision-making on particular moral issues. As we leave behind the discussion of the church as a bearer of moral tradition, it should be noted that this function serves as the middle term between the church as a shaper of moral identity and as a community of moral deliberation. The church as the locus and agent of tradition means the church provides material and setting for both character-formation and decision-making.

The Church as a Community of Moral Deliberation

As we just noted, the church functioning as a bearer of moral tradition overlaps with the church as a community of moral deliberation. Describing, assessing, and passing along moral tradition will inevitably entail moral deliberation and debate. People will reflect on their responsibilities in light of their moral convictions and commitments and will in one way or another raise those kinds of questions asked by critical and normative Christian ethics. The tradition will raise or address specific issues that lead not only to the question, "what ought we to do," but to that of "who we are and who we are to be." Thus concerns vital to Christian ethics are engaged when the church functions as a bearer of moral tradition.

Raising moral concerns in the church will also lead beyond the tradition. Influences and resources on any given issue will include those which are non-traditional and non-biblical. They will originate and have their life in cultural sources outside the orbit of the church. Genuine moral deliberation in the community of faith will be aware of these influences and resources and gather them from whatever quarter.

With these remarks as introductory we turn to a specific dimension of the church as a community of deliberation. We are referring to the church as "a community of moral discourse" [6] in the strict sense.

What does this mean? It refers to the kind of debate engaged in, whatever the issue. And what is the nature of that debate? An essay by Henry David Aiken on "the levels of moral discourse" [7] supplies a helpful description. We pause to explicate it while not losing sight of our main concern for the deliberative function of the church.

Aiken distinguishes four levels. On the first, people express judgments of value emotively, simply registering their feelings without reflection or deliberation. "Good job!" "Terrible move!" "You're bloody right!"

At the next level a reflective dimension emerges. "What ought we to do here" or "What should we have done" are typical questions. Appeal is made to resources that help answer the questions—precedents, principles, and data, for example. These are weighed in deliberative fashion and a reasoned case is made for different possible courses of action. This level of factual appraisal, reflection, and appeal for the practical purpose of determining action Aiken calls the "moral" level.

Often the reasons and resources employed on the moral level are themselves challenged. This elevates the discourse to the "ethical" level. For example, let us assume that on the moral level the question is asked, "What ought we to do here?" "We ought to do what most others have done in similar circumstances," is the answer given. A further question might then be posed: "On what grounds is the behavior of others sufficient basis for your own?" Or, if the answer to the "ought" question was "do what love demands," a further question might emerge: "What do you mean by 'love' and why is it the norm you use?" When the reasons and resources on the moral level come under this kind of scrutiny, "ethical" discourse characterizes the debate. That is, the rules, norms, guides, and gauges that people use, and the manner of practical reasoning they employ on the moral level, are subjected to critical assessment. They are called to account. Their justification is asked.

What happens when ethical discourse itself is pursued; when, for example, Christian normative ethics presents and defends the case for agapeic love as the supreme norm for morality? Eventually a level is reached where further reasons for and against come to an end and the conversation partners can do little more than declare to each other their last-stand convictions, assumptions and commitments and challenge each other to respond to them. They can only make clear the final beliefs and loyalties that underlie the cases made on the ethical level. Thus one partner might contend that love is the supreme norm because at the heart of Christian faith rests the conviction that God's very essence is love and humanity's supreme goal is communion with God and one another. If the other partner states she has found no grounds to believe God even exists, much less is love, or that human destiny is communion, then ethical discourse has come to an end. A "post-ethical" level is now the level of exchange. There is room only for stating and responding to ultimate convictions and commitments.

These are the levels of moral discourse—expressive, moral, ethical, and post-ethical. They are common to everyday exchanges. We continually intersect them when we deliberate moral matters. But why should the church as a gathered community concern itself with them? Why should it be "a community of moral discourse?" There are three reasons. The first two are applicable to other communities as well, the third is distinctive of the church.

The church should be such a community for the sake of the moral maturity and growth of its members. Some people handle moral issues on an emotive plane almost exclusively. They offer little more in the way of a reasoned response to "what ought we to do" than the response that a particular course "feels" right. Others are able to command resources at the moral level, knowing full well what ought to be done and for what "obvious" reasons. Yet the same persons may experience a paralyzing perplexity when their morality is challenged by the probing questions that "ethics" presses. Still others may experience a sense of no-ground-under-their-feet at the ethical and post-ethical levels because they are not clear about their fundamental beliefs and commitments. Or they are not clear about the connections to their morality and ethics of the beliefs and commitments they can identify as their own. When the task is that of critical ethics, challenging the morality of others, or even their own, they function altogether well. When it is that of normative ethics, they, too, may experience moral paralysis or feel themselves at the edge of an abyss.

One mark of moral maturity is the ability of persons to be conversant on all these levels. They can be if they know themselves, their feelings on moral matters, their moral and ethical reasons and resources, their post-ethical commitments and convictions. They can be if they know the examined life. Yet the requisite knowledge is not innate. It is acquired; and it is acquired in community, as gifts dependent on discourse are. What is required, then, is a community or communities which promote the moral maturity and growth of members by intersecting in a conscious way all these levels of discourse as moral issues are confronted and discussed. The church has often been, can and ought to be, such a community.

Helping to achieve moral maturity is not the only important function of moral discourse, however. Another is the fostering of full deliberation on any given issue, *for its sake*. It matters not just to the decision-maker, but to the decision itself what the feelings, the norms, the grounds and justification, and the ultimate contentions and assumptions, are. Disclosing these in a setting of public scrutiny and accountability is critical to fuller understanding and wiser choices and actions. This is the second reason why the church, as other communities, should promote moral discourse: thorough-going deliberation increases the chances for intelligent resolution of the moral issues themselves. The church has often been, and should continue to be, a community of moral discourse toward this end.

There is a third reason, one distinctive of the church. What we mean by the church as a community of moral deliberation is the church as the gathering of Christians for the explicit purpose of exploring and reflecting on their responsibilities, in light of their basic commitments and convictions as Christians and in view of the particular moral issues at hand in a given time and place. No other community brings precisely this identity founded in the Christian scriptures to bear on the moral issues at hand. Doing this well, however, means the church acting as a community of moral deliberation. It means consciously inquiring about the scriptural meanings not only on the moral level, but especially on the ethical and perhaps above all the postethical level. It means consciously engaging the Bible as authority throughout this range of deliberation. But it means above all simply supplying the ethos and environment in which the lines are discerned, drawn and secured between the identity *of* Christians and the stands taken *as* Christians on particular moral issues, the ethos and environment in which the circle of identity informing decisions and decisions forming character is closed and then initiated anew.

The church is, in summary, the chief community context for the Christian moral life. It will function as this context by being a community forming and reforming Christian moral identity; by providing moral tradition in which to stand and upon which to draw, and by serving as the appropriate environment for moral deliberation. Throughout the exercise of these functions the scriptures are indispensable, not only for the forging of the Christian moral life, but for the very notion of the church *as* church. Or, more pointedly stated for the concerns of this volume, part of what it means to be "church" at all is the relating of Bible and ethics in the moral life. At stake is Christian character and conduct and the life of the church as the people of God.

We are aware that the church is more than the sum of these functions, however. Even for Christian ethics it is more. We have not mentioned the patterns of the church's social engagement—those how and who questions—and that is a matter vital to ethics.[8] We have not discussed, in other words, the important function of the church as an agency of action. Yet we break off the discussion here in the hope that what has been said might be suggestive for what have lately been the more neglected understandings of the church in Christian ethics. We have sought to demonstrate the need for a fuller understanding of the church as both a necessary and decisive community for the Christian moral life. The aim has also been to provide the previous discussion of the tasks of Christian ethics with a description of the proper community setting for relating Bible and ethics. The next undertaking is to say more than we have about the church's scriptures, their authority and character and their availability for ethics done in this community.

5 biblical authority and non-biblical sources

At several points we have mentioned the problem of authority in relating the Bible to Christian ethics. What is the nature of biblical authority in making moral judgments? It is certainly clear that the Bible is not authoritative for Christian ethics at the point of making ethical decisions for us. Both the shaping of Christian character and the making of Christian ethical decisions involve many influences and sources of insight. What is their authority in relation to one another? It is time to address these questions directly.

Christians cannot escape the question of biblical authority because it is inherent in the claim that the Bible constitutes scripture for the church. It is not possible to regard the Bible as simply one of many possible influences or sources of insight in ethical matters. When the Bible is claimed as scripture by the church a special status or authority is being claimed for it. Scripture is understood as somehow normative for the life of the church and those individuals who identify with that historic community.[1] To be sure, there are many ways of understanding that normative character of scripture, but Christian ethics, since it shares the scriptural foundations of the church, is not free to regard the Bible as only one among a myriad of historic and modern cultural factors to be taken into account in the doing of Christian ethics. The particular authority of the Bible as the church's scripture must be considered.

The word authority refers to that which a community acknowledges as a source of decisive influence in its life. *An* authority may be a body of material (e.g. the Constitution), a person or a group of persons. In the church we speak of the authority of scripture as a way of referring to the acknowledged position of the Bible as normative for the Christian life. Authority is not a property inherent in the Bible. It is the recognition of the Christian community over centuries of experience that the scripture deserves central place as an authority for determining the character and conduct of Christians. Authority derives from acknowledgment of a source's right to influence us, not from absolute power that operates apart from the affirmation of the community. James Gustafson in a paraphrase of H. Richard Niebuhr wrote "authority . . . is the kind of power that is exercised over us by consent, and voluntarily negated by dissent." [2] To raise the question of biblical authority in matters of ethics is to ask, "What is the nature and degree of influence to be given the Bible in shaping Christian character and decisions in light of its continued acknowledgment by the historic church as scripture?"

In moral matters authority is not something possessed solely by scripture. The claim to be scripture establishes an authority for the Bible that must be taken into account, but its authority is not absolute. Many other sources of influence and insight become authoritative in moral deliberation. Historical perspectives, socio-economic data, scientific data, rational arguments and an endless variety of other non-biblical sources are authoritative in the making of particular moral judgments. The real question to be dealt with here is the relationship of biblical authority to the authority of non-biblical sources for Christian ethics. James Barr has helpfully suggested that the whole notion of authority is relational.[3]

> (Authority) is a relational or hierarchic concept; it tries to order and grade the various powers, or sources of ideas, that may influence us. . . . The notion of authority defines the priority of one such force over another. . . . Authority is used in an attempt to relate or to grade the forces bearing upon Christian belief and action.
>
> 'Authority' . . . thus defines relation. (It) defines i) the relation between the Bible and ourselves, so that the Bible may be seen as something binding upon us, something to which we have to submit ourselves; and ii) the relation between the Bible and other documents or sources of knowledge which might also influence our minds or actions at the same time.

It is well, however, to avoid from the beginning the notion that we can create a hierarchical order of influences on the Christian moral life and locate the position of scripture in absolute terms within the hierarchy. We have already seen enough of the way in which scripture functions in Christian ethics to know that this is not possible. We can suggest in advance of our discussion in this chapter that a more multi-faceted understanding of biblical authority is needed than has usually been espoused in the church. Most views of biblical authority have been too rigid to allow a dialogic relationship of biblical material with non-biblical material in moral judgments.

Authority and the Ongoing Activity of God

One of the classical ways of viewing biblical authority has been to relate it to the concept of inspiration. The Bible is authoritative because it is inspired. We need not get into the various positions discussing the way in which the Bible is an inspired book. All those who locate the authority of the Bible in its character as an inspired book share in common the view that the Bible is somehow directly from God in a way that other writings are not. James Barr points out that this view of inspiration tends to locate the importance of the Bible in its origins.[4] Because the Bible came into being as a result of the direct inspiration of God it is to be regarded as the central authority for faith and life in the church.

This viewpoint has been widespread in the church and still receives much attention in some circles. The implications for Christian ethics are far-reaching. Since the Bible constitutes the only document inspired of God the tendency is to make the Bible a self-sufficient authority for Christian moral judgments. God's will is revealed in the scripture, and it can then be used prescriptively to determine what we should do ethically. This position is reluctant to admit any real validity to moral insight gathered from non-biblical sources. This position also allows little flexibility in the way we regard the various materials of the Bible. Since the whole scripture is inspired it is equally authoritative, and this tends to imply that we use all biblical materials in the same manner when consulting it for ethical resources, although in fact this is seldom the case. In sum, the stress on inspiration makes the authority of the Bible inherent in the Bible itself, its origins and character. It disregards non-biblical materials as sources of ethical insight.

It is our contention that the question of biblical authority is not properly focused in the inherent character of the Bible itself. We believe the question is most fruitfully focused on God himself as he is active in the world and as his will is disclosed to persons in and through that activity. Here exegesis and ethics find a significant common ground. Both seek to discern the disclosure of God's will for his people. Exegesis strives to interpret the biblical record of God's self-disclosure to the communities of Israel and the early church in such a way that it illumines the church's understanding of God's activity and the revealing of his will for the present day Christian community. Christian ethics, faced with questions of how Christians are to understand and conduct themselves in a complex and changing world, seeks to read the signs of God's activity and to discern his will for the present, and in so doing calls on the resources of the historic Christian faith, including in primary position the scriptures and their history of interpretation in the church. In a sense exegesis moves from the historic witness to the present witness while Christian ethics begins with a present demand to be and do, and draws on the historic witness to meet that demand. But both activities are the necessary activities of the same community, the church. As such it is a travesty that the work of exegesis and ethics have been compartmented from one another.

The problem with locating biblical authority in the concept of inspiration is the narrowness of the view of God that results. It is as if God ceased to be active after the closing of the canon. The tendency is to speak as if God's disclosure of his will is limited to the past, and as if it is only in the written record of that past that his presence and will can be known. A strict view of inspiration leaves no room for the ongoing activity of God and the possibility that he might reveal himself through sources other than the Bible.

God was not only active in relationship to the biblical communities. He has continued to make his will known to the church in all succeeding ages, and he is still present, disclosing his will for the church and the world. The job of exegesis and ethics is to aid the church in discerning that will. This wider understanding of God's activity greatly opens the range of possibilities for theological and ethical sources of insight. The history of the church and its understandings of the faith, secular ideologies, the course of contemporary events, data from non-theological disciplines—all of these and many more become possible avenues through which God may confront us or inspire us with knowledge of his will for his creation.

There is, however, a danger here as well. In stressing the universal and timeless activity of God there is a danger of completely relativizing the Bible. There are those who regard the Bible as just one among many expressions of religious experience in the human community. All are to be regarded as authoritative in the same sense. This view takes seriously the on-going activity of God, but does not take seriously the uniqueness of the Bible's witness to that God.

The Nature of Biblical Authority

We can now make several observations about the nature of biblical authority in relation to the concerns of Christian ethics.

1. Whatever authority is to be ascribed to the Bible is authority *derived* from God who is truly absolute. The Bible is authoritative not in any absolute sense but in the sense that it records God's disclosure of himself to the community of faith. Authority refers to the revealing of God's will through the biblical witness. Thus, any form of biblicism is to be avoided as an abroga-

tion of God's freedom. Such biblicism worships the witness itself rather than the God of whom witness is offered.

2. The Bible does, however, possess a uniqueness. For those seeking to do *Christian* ethics the Bible has a special significance not shared by other sources of ethical insight. The Bible cannot be totally relativized as simply one among many sources of ethical insight.

First of all, it is the document which establishes the particular identity of the historic community called the church. The Bible is the record of the origins of the church and of the faith tradition it bears. In particular it is the only witness to the person and work of Jesus Christ who stands as the focusing center for the Christian faith and for the Christian moral life. Christian ethics is free to choose among the many sources of ethical wisdom available, but it is not free to ignore the scripture because it is the Bible that establishes the basic meaning of the word "Christian" in the phrase "Christian ethics."

Secondly, not only does the Bible serve to establish the historic identity of the church, but it provides a chief influence in shaping the perception of current ethical matters. Through the liturgy, proclamation, and teaching of the church the Bible influences the way in which the Christian community seeks to discern God's will in the world and to act on it. Since the Bible is constantly present in the life of the church, shaping Christian perception, it therefore influences the ability of individual persons of faith to find God's active will in other non-biblical sources. Only as the church comes to know God in its own historic traditions can Christians hear his voice or see his work in the present.

3. Does the uniqueness of the Bible mean that its authority in moral matters is absolute? We have already suggested that it does not. The authority of the Bible is a necessary factor in mak-

ing ethical judgments, but it is not self-sufficient. James Gustafson writes, "An authority can be unique without being exclusive. The Bible has such a status. . . . Thus, for Christian ethics, its authority is inescapable without being absolute." [5]

We would like to suggest that biblical authority in ethical matters be viewed in terms of primacy rather than self-sufficiency. By this we mean that among all of the possible sources of ethical insight the Bible stands out as primary but by no means totally adequate. It is primary because the church has throughout its history found the Bible to be a consistently reliable witness and guide to God's disclosure of his will both in biblical and subsequent times. Thus, its unique relationship to the church makes it the *constant* source to which the church must refer in the shaping of moral character and in the making of ethical decisions. For Christians no other sources of ethical wisdom can claim these characteristics. The primacy of the Bible as an authority for ethical judgment simply indicates its position as the single *necessary* reference point to be taken seriously in all ethical reflection within the church.

It is equally important to stress that although the Bible may be the primary authority it is not a sufficiently broad base of authority for making ethical judgments in the modern church. The Bible is a necessary source, but it must also be in constant dialog with the many other sources of knowledge and insight through which God might be disclosing himself.

The Bible itself anticipates this point. It has become clear that in the growth of the biblical material Israel and the early church did not hesitate to draw on sources already in existence outside their communities of faith if those materials served to communicate more clearly their understanding of relationship to God and his will for his people. Many elements of Israelite law and covenant seem to rely on well known international legal traditions. Wisdom literature is now widely understood as a secular genre characteristic of royal courts in the ancient Near East which Israel has borrowed and used to her own purposes. The author of the Gospel of John used a whole range of philosophic categories current in the Hellenistic world of his day to present his unique witness to the life of Jesus. The list could go on endlessly. It is sufficient to say that the Bible itself makes clear that the sources of theological and ethical insight are not narrowly limited to those materials that arise from within the community of faith itself.

This has continued to be true throughout the history of the church. St. Augustine found his theology and ethics profoundly influenced by neoplatonism, and St. Thomas Aquinas utilized the philosophy of Aristotle. It is no less true for our present day. The church cannot do ethics on the basis of the Bible alone. Within the church itself we are dependent on a long history of biblical interpretation and its related moral and theological tradition. Outside the church we must take account of the sociopolitical context in which ethical issues arise; we must heed the voices helping us to understand the cultural context in which the church seeks to shape moral character and discharge its mission to the world; we must avail ourselves of secular categories which aid the church in more effectively communicating its moral concerns. There are far more non-biblical sources available to the church in its exercise of ethical judgment than we could list here.

The task of the church then is to bring its unique resources based in the scripture into dialog with the many non-biblical sources of ethical insight. The Bible remains primary in its authority for this process because it is the key to distinguishing Christian ethics from ethics done in some secular mode.

4. It is important to recognize at this point that the Bible is

not claimed as a primary authority in Christian ethics on the basis of empirical, objective judgment about the Bible as an ethical source. The claim for biblical primacy is a confessional stance. Christian ethics because of its tie to the historic church is ethics which has committed itself to making ethical judgments within the framework of a community that recognizes the Bible as primary authority for its life.

An example will help make this clear. In both the Old and New Testaments there is a clear moral imperative to care for the poor and the hungry to the extent even of identifying with them and championing their needs. In the current debate about world hunger some have seriously advanced a position now labeled as "lifeboat ethics." [6] Some who hold this position argue that developed nations such as the United States occupy a limited number of positions in a hypothetical lifeboat. The lifeboat may be able to hold a few more, but it cannot accommodate all the people in a world of limited resources. The position then argues that our course of action must be to resist letting others aboard the lifeboat, by force if necessary, or otherwise, it will be swamped and we will all perish. Strong arguments can be made for this position as one of enlightened self-interest, hard-nosed but necessary. Whatever the virtues of this position it cannot be espoused by Christians taking up the issue of world hunger because it is in fundamental violation of a moral imperative clearly declared in the biblical witness and upheld by centuries of Christian tradition. Lifeboat ethics, to the extent that it is based on self-interest alone can be ruled out not on the grounds of objective argument, but because it is in fundamental opposition to the biblical framework within which Christian ethics takes its confessional stance.

5. Finally, we would like to suggest that any view of biblical authority adequate for Christian ethics must be functional.

Biblical materials are used in many different ways as a resource for Christian ethics. The problem with most discussions of biblical authority is that they seem to imply a monolithic view of the Bible and its use. There is no single way in which the Bible is authoritative in ethical matters. For example, a clear and consistent moral imperative within the biblical witness, such as the imperative to identify with and care for the poor, carries a definite authority in ethical discussions of poverty within the modern church. On the other hand, the biblical witness concerning attitudes toward marriage and sexuality is more diverse. There is no one biblical perspective, and yet the biblical materials still carry authority in that they set the necessary framework for the church's discussion of ethical issues in this area. The point to be made here is that biblical authority is functioning in different ways with different meanings in these examples.

Alan Verhey [7] has made a similar point when he distinguishes between the authority of scripture and what authorizes the move from scripture to moral claims. The authorizations which license moves from data to claim are called warrants. Persons may agree that scripture is authoritative but differ widely on appropriate warrants for moral claims. Our point, using Verhey's categories, is that different types and uses of biblical material may require differing sets of warrants. This is similar to our plea for a recognition that scriptural authority be seen as functioning in a variety of ways. An appeal to biblical authority as such does not settle the question of how biblical materials are to be used. This question is the functional one of proceeding from scripture to moral claim. In the next chapter we shall discuss in detail our understanding of this appropriation of biblical resources for different moral uses.

We suggest that biblical authority operates differently depending on the nature of the biblical materials that speak to a given issue. Further we wish to argue that such a functional view of biblical authority is necessary if the totality of the Bible's resources is to be made available to Christian ethics. It is a narrow definition of authority, implying the self-sufficiency of scripture, that has led to a narrowing of the biblical resources available to Christian ethics so that only passages explicitly addressing moral matters can be used.

Our treatment of biblical authority as primacy is intended to allow for a more flexible and functional view of biblical authority, and at the same time to stress the necessary biblical frame of reference within which ethical inquiry must take place if it is to be Christian. It might be well to conclude by making some remarks on how biblical and non-biblical resources would function both in the development of Christian moral character and in the making of ethical decisions in the life of the church.

The Bible and Non-Biblical Sources

1. One of the ethical tasks of the church, as we have seen, is the development of Christian moral character. Here we are talking about the shaping of the decision-maker rather than the decision. The church is charged with the long-range task of nurturing individuals within the particular framework of the Christian tradition. The ethical implications of this task are far-reaching since it affects the perspective and values that an individual brings to any concrete ethical decision.

In the development of Christian moral character the primary role of biblical authority seems clear. Here we might say that biblical primacy is substantive, by which we mean that biblical materials form the starting place and contribute the basic content for the shaping of Christian identity. Even the long theological and ethical tradition of the church can seldom be understood or appropriated aside from a basic understanding of the biblical witness that shaped it. The primary authority of the Bible in the formation of Christian character cannot be challenged because for many basic components of the Christian identity it is the *only* source. Most obvious is the Bible's role as the only witness to the life, death, and resurrection of Jesus Christ and the founding of his church.

There are, of course, other sources that contribute to the molding of moral character. Every person is influenced by familial ties, cultural influences, and personal relationships. We do not wish to underestimate the importance of these influences. But these influences shape moral character in general. None of these can become sources for the shaping of *Christian* moral character except as they might in particular instances point back to the particular understandings of the Christian faith which are grounded in the biblical witness.

The relationship between the Bible and non-biblical sources in this area is somewhat dialogic in that they influence each other. Cultural understandings enter into and affect our interpretation of the biblical witness such as the development in the late 19th century of critical methods in the study of the scripture. However, for the most part the relationship is not so much dialogic as transformational. The shaping of Christian character, in which the Bible plays a central role, transforms our apprehension of other shaping influences. The outcome of Christian moral development is the establishment of a basic Christian character grounded in biblical understandings of the faith which acts to focus and transform all of the other non-biblical sources for moral character development.

The primary role of biblical authority in this area is both substantive and transformational, and the church engages in both of these tasks. In its liturgy, preaching, and teaching the church attempts to bring the influence of the scripture alive in the formation of basic Christian character within the community of faith. It also seeks to show the Bible's role in transforming our perception and appropriation of other non-biblical sources of influence. This is sometimes implicit as in the telling of Bible stories to children that have obvious application to their own lives. At other times it is explicit as in the preaching of an exegetical sermon on a text with ethical implications that are pertinent to the struggles of the congregation.

It seems wise to utter a word of caution before moving on. Our claim for the transforming role of the Bible in relation to non-biblical sources is not a retreat back into absolute authority for the Bible. The many non-biblical sources of moral development are absolutely crucial. These sources allow the church to relate its message and mission to every age and culture. The Bible alone is not sufficient for the task of moral development. Without the influence of general cultural insights the church would become like some anachronistic sects attempting to recreate the cultural patterns of biblical times as if the world had not changed. We merely insist that for those who identify themselves as Christians biblical authority is primary for moral development because it forms the framework of Christian identity through which we receive and appropriate all other valuable knowledge and insight for the moral life.

2. In the area of ethical decision-making the starting point for the church is usually an issue that demands resolution. This usually means that non-biblical sources of ethical insight have come into play at the earliest point. In response to this ethical issue the church then seeks to bring its particular resources including the Bible to bear on the problem. For example, in the issue of world hunger a wealth of secular data had been amassed to

document the causes and proportions of the crisis before much significant response from the church had been generated. In this as in many instances the non-biblical material was instrumental in identifying the matter as an issue that demanded our attention in the first place. To cite another example, it was only after medical science began the actual use of organ transplants that it began to receive attention as an ethical issue. Further such ethical discussions can only take place in close relationship to the particular knowledge of medical technology.

The point to be made here is that in the area of decision-making the relationship between biblical and non-biblical sources is relational and dialogic from the beginning. In decision-making the interaction of biblical and non-biblical materials is almost always explicit.

The primacy of biblical authority in decision-making can be substantive as in the case of moral imperatives made clear in the biblical witness. Here the Bible contributes basic moral content which is intended as a part of the fundamental perspective of every member of the community of faith. In such instances those who engage in decision-making from a Christian perspective may draw on non-biblical insights and possibilities only if they do not violate the basic biblical imperative. We shall discuss such moral imperatives in greater detail in the following chapter.

More often the relationship of biblical authority to non-biblical authorities is not directly substantive. For many issues there is no one biblical position, and some issues are not directly addressed at all (e.g. ethical issues relating to modern technology). We would like to suggest that in such instances the primacy of biblical authority is not so much a direct source of content as an agent of control. Since the Bible is the *constant* source of insight for *Christian* decision-making, it serves as the controlling frame of reference within which we approach a decision. The biblical witness on a particular issue may show a radical polarity of positions; hence, it is within that polar tension that we must weigh all other sources of insight and come to a decision. The Bible may show a whole range of options on another issue. In this case we are alerted to consider this whole possible range of choices and the particular circumstances in which they might be made before we reach a decision. Even on an issue not explicitly addressed in the Bible we are called upon to consider our non-biblical source in light of applicable biblical principles such as justice for all persons.

Where values and decisions related to a particular issue are already formed and being urged on the church, biblical authority may play a corroborative role related to the controlling function we have been discussing. Christians analyze the content of secular ethical wisdom in light of the biblical witness seeking judgment on its claims. The Bible serves to validate or reject such claims in terms of their consistency with biblical truth claims and their expression in Christian moral character.

The function of biblical primacy in decision-making is to prevent the church from reaching decisions on the basis of non-biblical sources alone without reference to the insights of its own particular tradition. The Bible acts as a control agent to insure that Christian decision-making is dialogic—biblical faith interacting with the best wisdom of our modern world. Again it must be stressed that the Bible alone is not a sufficient basis on which to reach a decision with regard to most ethical issues. The authority of non-biblical knowledge and insight is crucial, but what distinguishes Christian from humanistic ethics is an insistence on the biblical witness as it has been handed down in the church as the primary authority establishing not the final word but the necessary framework for Christian moral deliberation.

3. We must briefly mention the obvious. The church's development of Christian moral character and its ethical decision-making are not sharply separated dimensions of the Christian moral life. These activities are going on simultaneously in the life of the church and constantly influence each other. Of special importance is our recognition that the Christian decision-maker brings to the decision a particular set of perceptions and values shaped by his conscious stance within the church. Thus, he must be ever aware that that stance alone gives the biblical witness primary authority in respect to all other sources of ethical insight. Decision-making is influenced by the formation of moral character, the formation of moral character is influenced by a long tradition of ethical decision-making, and both are grounded in the Bible as the primary but not exclusive authority for the Christian moral life.

6 making biblical resources available

In spite of general agreement that the Bible is an important resource for the church in dealing with ethical issues, the fact is that in practice its role is an insignificant one. Christian ethicists often acknowledge the Bible in chapters on biblical foundations, but its influence is meager within the pages of ethical discussion that follow. It seems ironic that in a time when critical scholarship has clarified so much in our understanding of the scriptures that the Bible actually seems less available as a resource for the Christian moral life. One can only speculate on the reasons for this. Perhaps the explosion of biblical knowledge has made the Bible seem complex and formidable. On the other hand, it may be that American life with its emphasis on immediate gratification has made church people unwilling to undertake the disciplined study of the Bible which might unlock its resources. The seeming urgency of ethical issues may stand in tension with the longer term nurturing of Christians in their own biblical inheritance so that the insights of those ancient communities might inform the decisions of the present.

This chapter is intended to suggest how the Bible might be made available as an ethical resource. Initially its concern is with two matters that seem largely ignored both by Christian ethicists and those in the local parish concerned with ethical issues.

1. Far too little attention has been paid to the distinct character of the Bible as the source of moral insight and guidance. The Bible is often consulted as if its unique character requires no special understanding. The results of such consultation are usually disappointing. Without understanding its nature the Bible may seem obscure, contradictory, and irrelevant.

Those dealing with an ethical issue may spend enormous amounts of energy investigating the socio-political factors of a given situation. Great attention is paid to characterizing and evaluating different types of data, and the tendency is often to stress the uniqueness of each situation. This makes it all the more interesting that if the Bible is consulted at all, it is somehow expected to speak directly to the issue as if it were a compendium of disembodied material having no character or context of its own. Our thesis is that to understand the character of the biblical witness is to crucially affect its use.

2. Even less attention has been given to a disciplined method for the study and use of the Bible. This is especially true in the local church where even the pastor may not be equipped to do basic exegesis of a biblical text. Many Christian ethicists concerned for method also display a lack of even basic exegetical tools. The fault lies partly in the guild of biblical scholarship in which critical study of the Bible has been defined in such a technical sense that it has become the province of the professional alone. We were told recently by a seminary faculty member that since exegesis of the Old Testament required the ability to read Hebrew he had ceased to teach exegetical method to seminarians. But the fault must also lie with a generation in the churches that is one of the least knowledgeable in the content of the scripture in the history of the church. It is possible to be an active church

member for an entire lifetime and still have no systematic knowledge of the Bible.[1] In the face of such monumental indifference it is little wonder that exegesis is becoming the sole possession of the scholarly guild.

We believe that if the church is to recover the Bible as an ethical resource, it can and must develop a capacity for disciplined reflection on the scripture. In short, it must learn to do its own basic exegesis. Further, the theological concerns the church brings to that task will yield insights not possible in the narrower framework of "objective" scholarly studies.

The Character of the Biblical Witness

It is not our intention to discourse at length on the unique character of the Bible. Whole volumes have been written on this. It is important, however, to note several aspects of the scripture which are particularly important and often overlooked in the use of the Bible as an ethical resource.

1. Most of those who have turned to the Bible for moral guidance have overlooked the *immense variety* of biblical literature which might be pertinent to ethical concerns. Since ethics in America has been issue-oriented the tendency has been to consult the Bible narrowly concerning what it says about a particular issue. Sometimes this has been broadened into exploring the biblical material on a key concept or ideal such as justice. The result is that the Bible's applicability to ethical issues has normally been limited to those portions of scripture which address ethical concerns directly. Passages that deal in moral exhortation have been the most consulted. Greatest interest has focused on law codes (especially the Ten Commandments), prophetic oracles of judgment, the ethical teachings of Jesus, and those epistles which address particular moral concerns in the early church.

In reality the Bible has a much greater range of resources for ethical insight than has usually been utilized. Many materials do not directly address issues that are important or even existent for us, but they witness to the efforts of the biblical communities in concrete historical circumstances to discover the will of God, and this forms the linch-pin of faithful deciding in any age. Narrative stories, historical events, wisdom sayings, parables, eschatological material, theological reflection, and liturgical material—all of these can yield ethical insight as well as passages that explicitly address ethical issues.

For example, the story of Jacob wrestling with the night visitor (Gen. 32:22ff.) does not seem on the surface to speak to ethical concerns. Jacob has up to this point lived a completely self-serving life. As a consequence, he is alienated from his own brother Esau, who has vowed to kill him. On the banks of the Jabbok River Jacob spends the night alone. He knows that on the next day he will meet his brother, and he does not know what fate awaits him. A man leaps upon him in the night and they struggle until dawn. It becomes clear that this is not an ordinary visitor. Jacob attempts to determine his own destiny again by wresting a blessing from the visitor, but instead he is humbled, his thigh is thrown painfully out of joint, and he is given a new name. Destiny was not in his control but in God's, and he names the place Peniel, ("face of God") because there he saw God "face to face" (32:30). But Jacob is a changed man. The conquest of his self-sufficiency, the finding of his new identity (in the naming), and even the inflicted pain which causes him to limp away, form the preconditions to genuine reconciliation with his brother Esau. He whom Jacob expected to encounter as an enemy is truly his brother, and on meeting Esau, Jacob says, "Truly, to see your face is like seeing the face of God" (33:10). Seen fully this text becomes one of profound pertinence

to ethical issues such as race. Those who were thought ene-
mies are brothers, and their reconciliation can only be through
the humbling and transforming (perhaps painful) of the brother
who has exploited the other.[2]

Or again, the eucharistic texts of the New Testament take on
new ethical significance when bread has become in our time not
simply a symbol of Christian community in Christ, but also a
symbol of division in the world between those who have bread
and those who must die for lack of it. A renewed exploration
of the brokenness of the bread and of Christ's body has deep
ethical implications for the church's response to global hunger.
But a narrow definition of ethical resources in the Bible would
not have included eucharistic texts.

A narrow selection of biblical material seems to have its origin
in an exclusive focus on decision-making. Since many ethical
decisions we must make are not directly addressed in the scripture it must indeed seem rather limited as an ethical resource.
We are suggesting that one key to making the Bible available
as an ethical resource is to see in its variety a wealth of insight
into the biblical values and norms that shape the life and commitment of those who make ethical decisions from within the
context of the community of faith.

2. In unlocking the biblical witness to ethical concerns it is
crucial that the *form and context* of a passage be given as much
attention as its content. The character of the Bible is such that
its materials generally speak in a very concrete form out of a
particular context in the life of the biblical communities. The
Bible is not given to generalized, universal address. Thus, it is
a travesty for church people and scholars to pick and choose
from the scripture as if its content could be directly applicable
apart from a serious consideration of form and context.

The sole focus on content has led to numerous distortions.

There are those who abstract the content of great themes such as covenant, justice, and the kingdom of God as if these were given no concrete reality in the Bible, and as if these themes could be appropriated apart from the struggles to understand them in a particular manner in a particular situation. There are those who fail to see that the same content may take on different meaning in different situations. For example, the story of Adam and Eve in Genesis 2-3 is of human freedom and the responsibility of the man and the woman to bear the consequences of their decision. In 1 Timothy 2:13-15 the story is used to indicate a subordinate sinful status for women. Those who consider only content often spend great amounts of energy trying to harmonize differences that could be understood in terms of form or context.

Attention to the form and context of biblical material serves the negative purpose of preventing hastily drawn analogies between biblical experience and our own. But it may also serve the more positive function of looking beyond the content of a passage on a particular issue to patterns of response used by the faithful community in many concrete situations. Beyond the prophetic indictments against various forms of social injustice lies a very concrete understanding of covenant. The form of their speaking betrays the covenant as a reference point although it is seldom mentioned directly. And the context in which the prophetic movement developed speaks of the demand of the covenant for those who speak God's word despite the prevailing patterns of society. The ethical implications of this theme of covenant concretely revealed in the form and context of their speaking far transcend the individual issues to which they speak.

3. In both the Old and the New Testaments *doing is intimately tied to being*. Those with ethical concerns most often approach the Bible asking, "What shall I do?" The Bible resolutely tells

us that what we do is dependent on who we are called to be. We are called to be the faithful community of the people of God. It is out of this identity that we are to decide and act. The tendency is to seek help in deciding on an ethical issue without responding to the summons into relationship with God through the community of faith.

The Bible is clear that to know God's will is to do it. These are not elements that can be separated from one another. The presupposition is relationship to God. "He has showed you, O man, what is good; and what does the Lord require of you but to do justice, and to love kindness, and to walk humbly with your God?" (Micah 6:8). Here relationship to God is made inseparable with the doing of justice. When Jesus characterizes the great commandment as love of God and love of neighbor he is also implying this dual reality in the life of faith, that relationship to God is the corollary of service to the neighbor. "Be doers of the word, and not hearers only" (James 1:22). This should not send us off in a frenzy of mindless activity even in the best of causes. It should tell us that discerning God's will and doing it are necessarily related.

The biblical materials were preserved by the community of faith for a particular purpose. The Bible spoke the Word anew in each generation calling men and women into the relationship of faith. Those who ignore this dimension do not find in the Bible a very helpful source of ethical insight. Some study the Bible only as a historical document of the church's roots, and hence find it irrelevant to the present. Others ask it to make decisions for them and are disillusioned when it often fails to do that.

The Bible itself tells us we cannot separate being and doing. Thus, if the Bible is to be a resource for the moral life we must give up an excessive focus on the ethics of doing. We must ask

"Who am I to be?" before we ask "What shall I do?" Of course, our deciding and acting can be informed by the scripture, but not apart from its role in forming the basic identity and character of those (individually and corporately) who do the deciding and acting from within the relationship of faith. We shall return to these matters at later points.

We have traced three elements in the character of the biblical witness that are important in approaching the Bible as an ethical resource: the immense variety in biblical literature, the importance of form and context, and the intimate relation of being and doing. Now we must turn our attention to more concrete methods for unlocking the resources of particular texts.

The Importance of Exegesis

If the Bible is to serve as an ethical resource there must be some disciplined method for understanding and explaining the meaning of biblical texts. In most churches the Bible is consulted on a haphazard basis. If the text consulted seems understandable on the surface it may be used and have some influence. If the message of a text is not immediately apparent it will be dismissed or perhaps not even discovered in the first place. The Bible is the complex record of the biblical communities in their relationship to God over a period of more than a thousand years. As such the Bible could not be expected to be a self-interpreting document and yet, church people invest little systematic effort at understanding its message. If the Bible is to be made available to ethical concerns then persons in the churches must learn the basic fundamentals of exegesis.

Exegesis, according to the American Heritage Dictionary, is "a critical explanation or analysis; especially, interpretation of Scriptures." It is derived from two Greek words *ex* meaning "out" and *hegeisthai* meaning "to lead, or guide." It is the word commonly used in biblical studies to indicate the process of critically explaining a text, drawing out its meaning. The tools and techniques of exegesis have been developed extensively. But exegesis is a word rarely found in the vocabulary of persons in the local parish, and the process it represents is usually absent as well.

Somehow the idea has gotten abroad that exegesis is a task so complex that it is to be reserved for the specialist, the biblical scholar. In our experience there are even many pastors who suggest that the explication of biblical texts is a task beyond their skills. They want books and articles to perform this task for them, thereby telling them what to preach and teach. One of the fundamentals of the Reformation dealt with the right of the whole church, clergy and lay, to work at the interpretation of scripture. It would be ironic if, in our time, the interpretation of scripture became the province of only those few in the scholarly guild of biblical studies. As it is today, church people are seldom expected to enter into the process of disciplined reflection that exegesis requires. They are not asked to master the resources of their own faith tradition.

But it is our contention in this section that a mastery of basic exegetical skills is possible for any serious inquirer. We also contend that such mastery is necessary if biblical resources are to be available to the church in facing the ethical challenges of this day. We can now proceed to discuss various aspects of basic exegesis.

The first task of exegesis is to *examine the text*. For the average church member this cannot be done in the original language so one must rely on translations. Fortunately many excellent translations are available. The Revised Standard Version, the Jerusalem Bible, The New English Bible, The New American Bible and Today's English Version are but a few that might be used with profit. When congregations are working on biblical materials it is helpful to have several different translations present for comparison.

When translations are compared several things might happen. If the translation of a text varies radically from one version to another you might assume that serious translation problems exist, and translators have exercised differing judgments. This would certainly mean that one must be cautious in using a single translation of that text as a strong basis for some ethical stance. To make a judgment on which translation seems more probable one might have to consult commentaries or other helps. In any case, the caution flag should be out.

If the translations differ but not in ways that change the substance of the passage then the group working on the text is simply enriched by a wider variety of possibilities for expressing and making a passage communicate in translation. One of these may seem clearer and more illuminating than another and might then become the basic text for moving on to discuss its implications for the moral life.

Translations may differ on some key word. This may then focus study effort into a particular channel in an effort to illumine some key concept. For example, in the commandment "You shall not kill" some translations have said "You shall not murder." Does this verse refer to all taking of life, including war and self-defense, or does it refer to a narrower range of offenses as implied by using the word murder? Further inquiry would be needed, and the translation comparison would indicate the direction of that inquiry.

The by-product of careful attention to the text in using the Bible as an ethical resource is that even brief experience with the use of differing translations teaches the dangers of absolutizing any one biblical translation. Groups learn immediately that the

Bible is not a manual of moral information to be mechanically applied. Even to discover what the text says requires disciplined, reflective judgment. Hopefully this learning will carry over into discovering what the text means.

Once the text of a biblical passage has been investigated the exegete turns to a careful and critical discovery of the meaning of the text, insofar as that is possible. If the Bible is truly to become available as a resource for the Christian moral life, its passages must be understood as thoroughly as possible, both in the literary form by which they communicate with us and in the concrete historical circumstances which produced them. Since we wrote earlier on the importance of form and context in understanding the Bible we need not argue the point here. We can turn directly to the manner in which exegesis operates.

It is usually best to begin by examining the *literary style and organization* of a passage. Exegesis might be understood as a process of seeking answers to the particular questions raised by a given text. What type of literature is represented by the text? As it is organized where does the emphasis fall? Is there a logical stylistic structure to the passage? Is the passage part of a larger piece of material? How does it relate to that larger literary context (e.g. is it the climactical point of the whole piece)? Can anything be said about authorship? Are there direct literary parallels to the passage (e.g. a Gospel story or teaching might appear in three or four retellings)? Does the emphasis change among these parallels?

Closely related to literary questions are *questions of form or genre*. Many times the formal structure of a passage is of a distinct type that in itself tells us something about the meaning of the text and its use. Examples might be prayers, oracles of judgment, parables or visions. Without knowing the specific content of a passage we would begin to know something about it by being told it was one of these distinct genres. Many such genres have been distinguished in the Old and New Testament. The exegete must ask if the passage falls into any distinct formal category that allows it to be classed with a particular genre. If so, how does this affect our understanding of the passage's use in the biblical communities? How does it affect the way in which the passage speaks its message?

In raising *questions of historical context* about a passage we are really seeking to understand the life experiences of Israel or the early church which lie behind the text. There are often two levels of historical context with which the exegete must be concerned. The first is the concrete historical experience witnessed to directly by the text. For example, there is the central experience of the resurrection. Secondly, there is the historical context to which this witness was intended to speak. Although there was only one resurrection each Gospel directs its witness to a different period and set of circumstances in the life of the early church.

To take an Old Testament example, Isaiah 40-55 constantly uses the language of exodus. We therefore need to understand the experience of the exodus event as fully as possible. But the prophet is writing during the Babylonian exile, and we are also called to an understanding of the tragedy of that experience. Then we can see that the prophet has taken the experience of the exodus and by placing it in the context of his own exilic experience has transformed it into the hope of a new exodus. In making the Bible available for Christian ethics it is crucial that we see how a passage functioned in its own historic circumstances. The Bible can only come alive to our ethical concerns if we understand how it was alive for the communities of faith where it originated.

Finally, we may raise *theological questions* to the text. In light of its literary and historic contexts what is the theological message of the passage? What are its main theological motifs? What are the larger theological themes to which this passage relates? Are there key words or concepts that point to theological underpinnings which go beyond this passage? What was the theological importance of this passage to the biblical community of its time?

It is important to note that persons doing exegesis in the local church are not without helpful tools. There are many excellent commentaries, Bible dictionaries, Bible atlases, handbooks of biblical theology, and introductions to biblical literature. One should, however, avoid consulting these immediately. Before using these tools the exegete should carefully examine the passage under consideration and determine what are the significant questions which must be addressed. Then, reflecting on the text, begin to form initial judgments on the literary, historical and theological dimensions of the text. At this point one consults the available tools for assistance in reaching the fullest understanding of the passage.

Having examined a passage in its immediate context the Christian exegete must also take note of the full range of a passage and its themes in the entire canon. The church considers both the Old and New Testaments as scripture; therefore, a boundary for exegesis cannot be drawn between them. Specific passages or their related themes must be seen in their complete development in the whole canon. We shall return to the importance of the canon in detail in the next section. Suffice it at this point to indicate that the indispensable tool for this effort is a concordance. A concordance lists key words alphabetically and records every instance where that word appears in a biblical passage. Every serious student of the Bible whether scholar, clergy or laity should practice the use of a concordance. Not to do so is to look at a biblical text with blinders on thinking that what one sees immediately before him is all there is to see.

Those who define the task of exegesis narrowly as the descriptive task of the objective historian would conclude the discussion of exegetical method at this point. The text and its original meaning have been described as fully as possible. For the church this is not enough. Exegesis in the church must go beyond mere description to reflect on how the words of the biblical text become the Word of God which addresses his people anew in our time. The church's exegete must ask how a passage, fully and critically understood, lays its claim on the contemporary community of faith. What insight or guidance is given there for the church in its current struggles to be the faithful people of God?

In this final step the Bible becomes fully available as a resource for the church's ethical concerns. The Bible's application to ethical issues is not mechanistic; it is dialogic. One pole of the dialog is the situation out of which our current ethical concerns grow. The other pole is a full understanding of the biblical witness as we recover it through disciplined, exegetical reflection. Only as the biblical voices become fully audible can the dialog take place. The relationship between the Bible and ethical concerns then becomes a dynamic one in which there are many options whereby the scripture might influence Christian moral life. Without careful exegesis the biblical witness is not fully heard, and the contemporary pole of the dialog becomes a monolog confirming its prejudgments by picking and choosing from scriptures that have not been allowed to speak with their own voice.

This call to develop the capacity for exegesis in the local church is not an attempt to impose a narrow methodology. There is room for considerable variety in exegetical style. It is a call for the church to engage in disciplined reflection on its own scriptural resources. Only through such disciplined and systematic understanding of the biblical materials can the Bible properly function as a source of moral insight in the church.

The Canon as a Framework of Control

In the above discussion we have suggested that the task of exegesis is not completed until a text and its themes have been considered within the full range of the Christian canon. This has not been a customary viewpoint. Under the widespread influence of the critical method the tendency has been to analytically dismantle passages. Seldom has the theological meaning of the whole been given much attention. This is particularly true with respect to large bodies of biblical material. For example, is it not important that the oracles of an eighth century prophet named Isaiah and the oracles of an anonymous sixth century exilic prophet are preserved together in the same biblical book? Are not the different Gospel portraits to be read in relation to one another? Even more important, does the concept of the canon not imply that we are to read the New Testament in light of the Old Testament and vice versa?

Recently attention to redaction-criticism (the critical understanding of influences shaping whole biblical books or literary traditions) has brought some new interest to this area. At the same time there has been renewed interest in the meaning of the canon. Brevard Childs has been the most prominent voice in arguing that "the canon of the Christian church is the most appropriate context from which to do Biblical Theology." [3] We believe that he is right, and that the wider framework of the canon is of particular importance in appropriating biblical materials for Christian ethics. After a brief discussion of the wider canonical framework we will suggest that the canonical context acts as a control in several ways over the manner in which biblical resources are made available for ethical concerns.

The concept of the canon (and the word itself) are not familiar to many church people. Basically the word "canon" is used in the

Christian tradition to refer to that collection of books judged by the church to be authoritative for Christian life and doctrine. The word itself seems to come from a Semitic root meaning "rod" and derivatively "a measure." Thus, the biblical canon is a theological measure in the on-going tradition of the church.

Two basic observations on the nature of the Christian canon must be made. First, the clear understanding of the church is that the Christian canon is composed of both Old and New Testaments. Both together form the scripture of the church. This is particularly important since many in the church have tended to separate the two testaments. At best the Old Testament has been regarded as second-class scripture. Exclusive focus on the New Testament has truncated the traditional witness of the church that the whole scripture is the Word of God. This leaves the New Testament cut off from much of its rootage and impossible to be fully understood. From the point of view of the church's ethical concerns it vastly narrows the range of available resources and creates a false and narrow context for understanding the rest. Many noted works in Christian ethics deal with biblical foundations by treating only the New Testament.[4] Concern for the canon as the total framework for our biblical reflection acts as a corrective to this arbitrary narrowing of resources.

Here we might note that, although for Christians Jesus Christ is the focusing center for faith and ethics, there is no single understanding of his life and work that can give a simple, monolithic standard of moral judgment. Indeed, it is increasingly clear that to understand Jesus requires not only the diverse witnesses of the New Testament to his life and work, but the rich faith heritage of the Old Testament which provided foundation for Jesus' own understanding and proclamation of the good news that God had acted to redeem his people. The church has preserved the canon not as mere historical documentation but as necessary to the full understanding of its faith albeit centered in Jesus Christ.

A second observation is that the Christian canon should not be regarded as books which the church chose and granted authority. The church has always stressed that the complex process of the formation of the canon represented only the recognition by the church of authority from God already established in the life of the church. "The concept of canon was an attempt to *acknowledge* the divine authority of its writings and collections. . . . In speaking of canon the church testified that the authority of its Scriptures stemmed from God, not from human sanction." [5] This perspective provides a safeguard against the notion that the church, having made the canon, can therefore redo it, leaving out those portions which some regard as out-dated or irrelevant. In the principle of the canon the church acknowledges all of the Old and New Testament as possessing the authority of God's Word. In matters of ethics this means that we are not free to disregard the totality of scripture as in some way authoritative for the Christian moral life.

In our earlier discussion of authority we stressed that the authority of scripture is not absolute. Other factors enter into moral judgment. Here we would particularly wish to stress that in the immense variety of biblical materials, our own subjective judgments are bound to play a role in the selection of scriptural resources. In fact, our dialogic understanding of the process of appropriating scripture would require it. But the principle of canon insures that our subjective ethical dispositions be tested out on the broadest possible scriptural framework. We are forced to take seriously those scriptural materials that disagree with our judgments as much as those which agree. Our subjectivity is not replaced by some objective scriptural standard. The Bible is not such a monolithic document. Our subjectivity is to operate in the framework of control provided by the whole canon. Let us see how the canon might function in that way.

The importance of the canon in the Christian tradition means that any person who seeks to do exegesis within and for the church must do it in the context of the total canon. We have already stated above that this means a passage cannot be understood only in its own immediate context. Exegesis for the church cannot be defined narrowly. The understanding gained in study and reflection or any given passage must be brought into conversation with the full range of materials in the Christian canon, Old and New Testaments. The exegete must first ask if that passage is explicitly referred to in any other place in the Bible. If so, how does the tradition function there? Is it similar or different from the initial text? If the passage is not referred to explicitly are there places in the Old or New Testament where similar language is used? Or are there places where similar concepts and subject matter are taken up? [6] When the full range of pertinent material is before us we can then seek to see the dynamic relationships between materials within the Bible itself. A passage seen by itself might appear quite different in meaning and significance when seen alongside a much wider range of related biblical material.

Implications for Christian ethics are obvious. One cannot with integrity enter dialog with the scripture over ethical issues if the biblical warrants appealed to are narrow selections that have not been tested against the totality of the biblical witness. Of course, to do exegesis in the context of the canon runs the risk of discovering tensions and contradictions in the biblical material rather than a uniform moral witness. One can no longer cite only that pole of the tension most compatible with a position reached on other grounds. The canon often forces those who come to the Bible for moral guidance to face these tensions directly as a part of the ethical struggle. We might suggest that often these tensions prove to be present in the contemporary ethical situation and need to be faced there as well.

* * *

At this point it might be helpful to interrupt our discussion and briefly demonstrate with a particular text having ethical implications how a broader canonical context can change our understanding of a passage.

Matthew 23:6-13 tells of an incident in which a woman approaches Jesus and pours a jar of expensive ointment on his head. The disciples are scandalized by such waste and complain that money for the ointment could better have been given to the poor. Jesus intervenes by saying, "Why do you trouble the woman? For she has done a beautiful thing to me. For you always have the poor with you, but you will not always have me." He goes on to treat the anointing as a foreshadowing of his preparation for burial.

Jesus' statement, "For you always have the poor with you," has been a constant nemesis to those in the church who have tried to arouse the conscience of Christians in regard to the harsh realities of poverty both in our society and in the world. Those who have defined the gospel solely in terms of individual salvation use this text to justify a total lack of concern for the victims of poverty and the establishment of a just social order. They maintain that this text proclaims the futility of seeking to relieve the condition of the poor and focuses attention instead on the person of Jesus. To them this means the elevation of spiritual needs over material needs.

Indeed, if our exegesis is limited narrowly to this text we would not have much basis to argue against this point of view. Jesus does rebuke the disciples in their desire to give to the poor. He does turn attention to his own person. But does Jesus really intend that we should not be concerned with the material needs of those who suffer? Is attention to Jesus' own person a turning to totally spiritual matters? When we move to a wider canonical context our understanding of this passage begins to alter.

The first move is naturally to the wider description of Jesus' ministry in the Gospels. From the very beginning Jesus identified his ministry with the poor and the oppressed. In Luke 4:16-19, at the inauguration of his public ministry, Jesus preaches at Nazareth and chooses as his text Isaiah 61:1-2:

> The Spirit of the Lord is upon me, because he has anointed me to preach good news to the poor. He has sent me to proclaim release to the captives and recovering of sight to the blind, to set at liberty those who are oppressed, to proclaim the acceptable year of the Lord.

Jesus often associated himself with the poor and with society's outcasts and was criticized for it (Matt. 11:19; Luke 7:34). In his preaching, Jesus often spoke with concern for the poor and indicated that they were especially blessed by God (Luke 6:20-21). Perhaps most striking is the passage on the great judgment in Matthew 25:31-46:

> I was hungry and you gave me food, I was thirsty and you gave me drink, I was a stranger and you welcomed me, I was naked and you clothed me, I was sick and you visited me, I was in prison and you came to me.

Jesus makes clear that his very person is identified with the poor and the needy to the extent that acceptance of him is equated with ministering to their needs. "Truly, I say to you, as you did it to one of the least of these my brethren, you did it to me."

In light of the strong witness elsewhere in the Gospels to Jesus' concern with the material needs of the poor we surely cannot understand Jesus' statement in Matthew 26:11 to be a repudiation of his own ministry. Jesus is focusing attention in this passage on his own passion, but would not be urging that we ignore the needs of the poor and needy.

Moving more widely in the canon we find in Deuteronomy 15:7-11 a text with a statement so similar to that of Jesus that it raises the possibility that Jesus is directly referring to it. This passage is a part of the law, the Torah, which was well known to Jesus and many Jews of his time. The passage is making clear that concern for the poor is obligatory in the community of faith.

> There will be no poor among you . . . if only you will obey the voice of the Lord your God. . . . If there is among you a poor man, one of your brethren, in any of your towns within your land which the Lord your God gives you, you shall not harden your heart or shut your hand against your poor brother, but you shall open your hand to him and lend him sufficient for his need. . . . You shall give to him freely, and your heart shall not be grudging. . . . *For the poor will never cease out of the land;* therefore, I command you, You shall open wide your hand to your brother, to the needy and to the poor. . . .

This passage suggests that if the demands of the covenant were fully embodied there would be no poverty, but since Israel, like all human communities, is a "stiff-necked people," some of its inhabitants will inevitably be poor. Therefore, God's people are commanded to care for them. This task is part of what it means to be the people of God and it is not an optional activity.

This greatly alters our consideration of Matthew 26:6-13. Jesus is responding not to the disciples' desire to give to the poor, but to their rebuke of the woman. He is reminding them that the existence of the poor is a constant judgment against the whole covenant community. The woman is not to be self-righteously singled out; the poor are a corporate responsibility. By calling attention to the constant presence of the poor Jesus is not urging us to forget their needs. He is directly referring to God's command that we care for the poor. It is because they are always present that we do have a responsibility. Jesus then goes on to use the woman's gift to focus attention on his own passion, his own ultimate involvement in human suffering.

A wider canonical context completely alters our view of this passage. If we had searched more broadly we would have found even more texts relating the people of God to the welfare of the poor (the prophets, Paul). Far from allowing anyone to narrowly interpret Matthew 26:6ff. as elevating spiritual over material needs, an exegesis in the context of the whole scripture would have overwhelmed the exegete with the power of the moral imperative regarding the poor and needy.

* * *

It might now be suggested that in using the Bible as a resource for Christian ethics the canon acts as a framework of control in several important ways.

1. The canon serves to stress the crucial role of the community of faith in appropriating biblical resources. The canon grew out of the life experience of Israel and the early church in discerning the will of God. The church's recognition of the whole canon as authoritative implies the continuity of those communities. Thus, the canon means that the church is the appropriate context within which the Bible is made available to modern ethical concerns. It cannot be interpreted with integrity by individuals in isolation from the wider community of faith.

2. The canon also reminds us of the on-going activity of God.

When we must relate to the whole sweep of scripture we see God revealing himself in ever new ways within the Bible itself. Although every portion speaks with authority of God's presence as it was apprehended in a particular time and place, it is clear that no word is the final word concerning God's revealing of himself. The scripture points beyond itself to the reality of God. Faith understands that same God as active in our present. Thus, the canon encourages a dialogic use of scripture, not to discover God enshrined in the past, but to assist us in discerning his activity and will in our own day.

3. As a corollary to the previous point, the canon helps prevent the absolutizing of the biblical text. The biblical words are not to be worshiped as such (a practice sometimes called bibliolatry). Exegesis in the context of the canon shows the sweep and variety within the scripture and guards against the absolutizing of any one expression within the Bible. It teaches that the nature of the biblical word is dynamic and not static, thereby suggesting that in ethical matters we cannot seek to apply it mechanically.

4. The canon prevents the selecting of texts for ethical use based on the predisposition of the selector. The canon's stress on the wholeness of scripture means that ethical judgments cannot be based on marshalling only those texts that bolster a position already reached on other grounds. Even when it presents us with difficult tensions and contradictions attention to the canon requires that the totality of the biblical witness be weighed in reaching moral judgments. To pick out some portions as relevant and to reject others is to create one's own canon. Ethical statements based on such a limited canon are more often than not misleading. To do Christian ethics is to enter dialog with the whole of the Christian canon recognized as authoritative throughout the history of the church.

5. Finally, emphasis on the canon helps avoid critical reductionism. The tendency in critically analyzing biblical texts is to focus on the parts and to fail to see their relationships in the whole. Concern for the canon constantly calls the critic back to the dynamic interrelationship of the whole scripture. This does not mean a repudiation of critical methods, it simply implies a constant concern to move beyond criticism to discover the address of the Word, and this can never be done by simply looking at the critical results of examining a single text or even a single book. In seeking moral guidance this broader framework is essential.

If the Bible is made available through understanding its character, and through careful exegesis of its passages in the context of the whole canon then it can become a rich resource for the Christian moral life. We turn to a discussion of ways in which the Bible can act as such a resource.

The Bible as a Resource for the Moral Life

One of the mistakes often made in discussing the relation of the Bible to Christian ethics is to suggest a single, multi-purpose model for how scripture is to be used, such as moral law, moral ideal, or moral analogy. As the previous discussion suggests, this ignores the multi-faceted nature of biblical resources. It also suggests a monolithic character for ethical concerns in the church. We wish to suggest that there are several ways in which the Bible might appropriately function as a resource for Christian moral life.

1. The Bible acts as a shaper of Christian identity. It is the prime source of the self-conscious identity of the community of faith, and thus, of those individuals who choose to identify themselves with the church and its faith tradition. The Bible is the

witness of Israel and the early church to their struggles to be the faithful community of the people of God. It tells of their response to God's revealing of himself in their concrete life experience. In recognizing this witness as authoritative the church has established the self-understanding of those biblical communities as the normative guide for the church's attempt to be the faithful community in our own time. For those concerned with Christian ethics this means that the Bible is a primary source for those basic beliefs, values and attitudes which give Christians a particular identity which they share with the wider community of the church. In facing ethical issues this use of the Bible informs the perspective Christians bring to the issue. In simple terms, this use of the Bible refers to the shaping of the decision-maker rather than the decision.

If the Bible acts to shape basic identity, it should be apparent that this is not a function which can be left until an ethical dilemma presents itself for decision. This use of the Bible requires the long term nurturing of the community of faith by those responsible for ordering its life. If the distinctive beliefs, values, and attitudes of the church have not already been internalized from study and reflection on the biblical resources then it will not be possible to draw upon them meaningfully in the midst of moral and ethical crisis. The starting place for this function is not a defining ethical issue but the Bible itself. It is to be studied for its own basic witness to the shape of Christian moral character, as well as studied for its practical application to some particular moral issue.

In this function it should also be clear that the entire canon acts as a resource. The scripture in its entirety acts to mold moral character in the individual and in the community. Thus, stories are as ethically important as commandments; psalms are as influential as teachings. The basic character of the church is shaped by reflecting on the whole range of experience recorded in the scripture. Ethical significance is not limited to texts that explicitly address moral concerns.

For example, the Gospels are filled with stories that tell of Jesus' associations with those considered to be outcasts and sinners by others in the society of his time. Completely apart from any explicit instruction, the witness of these stories shape the kind of community the church is called to be; inclusive, accepting, renewing. The person who brings these attitudes to ethical situations dealing with poverty or criminal justice will find his decisions transformed.

Or again, those whose nurture in the biblical tradition has shown them the love songs of the Song of Songs as well as the more somber opinions of Paul on marriage will approach questions of sexual ethics with a sense of the possibilities for fullness as well as the dangers inherent in human sexuality.

Basic attitudes such as the Hebrew affirmation of creation as good or the Pauline conviction on the universality of the gospel have become fundamental to the perspective the church brings to ethical concerns. But these attitudes do not stay strong and sharp apart from their nurture at the well-springs of the Bible itself. Thought of in this way the ongoing study of the Bible and reflection on its wisdom in the church is an essential element in the church's moral life.

2. The Bible can act as the giver of moral imperatives. Here we are speaking of those areas in which the Bible speaks to us by means of direct moral address indicating an ethical stand which is not optional to those who are the people of God. Many ethicists and church leaders, in their desire to counter the use of the Bible as a prescriptive moral code, have tended to limit the function of the Bible to the setting of ideals or to entering a relational moral dialog as a resource. This glosses over the fact

that the Bible sometimes acts as the source of direct moral imperative. Both Old and New Testaments consistently affirm Jesus' summary of the greatest commandment, "You shall love the Lord your God with all our heart, and with all your soul, and with all your mind . . . and you shall love your neighbor as yourself" (Matt. 22:37-39). Thus, it is required of those who would love God that they put the welfare of their neighbor on a par with their own. This imperative profoundly affects any approach to ethical problems.

With such moral imperatives there is no need to wait for a specific issue to arise. The imperative is to be internalized as such. The church's stand in these matters is firmly established in the biblical material, although it must be stressed that considerable latitude will no doubt remain in regard to strategy and implementation of that stand. It should be obvious that such moral imperatives are closely related to our previous function of the Bible as the shaper of Christian identity. Indeed, our distinction here is an artificial one. The moral imperatives made clear in the biblical witness are to be internalized as part of the basic identity of the community of faith. We have separated them only because we were speaking previously about the shaping of values and attitudes, and here more directly about the identification of a particular moral stand.

A more extended example may be helpful at this point. In light of the world food crisis and the tragedy of global hunger the church has been wrestling with its response to this complex area of ethical concerns. Examination of the biblical materials shows a clear and unambiguous word on the relation of the community of faith to hunger and poverty. In the Old Testament God especially loves and cares for the poor (Ps. 10:12; 12:5; Isa. 25:4; 29:19). He does not accept their condition but promises to deliver them (Ps. 132:15; Prov. 15:15). Because God has identified himself with the poor, so too the community of faith is called to special concern for these persons. The rights of the poor are established in the law codes. Poverty is a judgment on the community's distribution of resources, and concern for the poor cannot, therefore, be left to voluntary benevolence. The prophets become the strong advocates of the poor and the oppressed, and urge this as the concern of the whole covenant community.

In the New Testament we have already noted above Jesus' radical identification with the poor and the oppressed,[7] and he commanded his followers to take up this concern as essential to discipleship. The early church shared all material resources in order to provide for the needy (Acts 2:44-45). Numerous references in the epistles indicate that identification with and concern for the poor remained a central imperative for the early church (2 Cor. 8:9; 9:9; Heb. 13:16; James 2:1-7).

The witness of both Old and New Testaments makes clear that concern for those forced to live a marginal existence in hunger and poverty is not an optional activity for the people of God. Nor is it only a minor requirement to be dealt with in token charities. Identification with these persons is at the heart of what it means to be the community of faith. A clear moral imperative is established in this area for those who would be the church.

A final word of caution is necessary. The church must constantly guard against those who would declare moral imperatives in areas where the biblical witness does not warrant this. The history of the church is filled with examples of those who endowed some limited portion of scripture with absolute moral authority. Careful exegesis in the context of the entire canon is the safeguard. When a moral concern is expressed in biblical materials that range from law codes to teaching narratives to parables to epistles then its demand is necessarily stronger than a concern expressed in a more limited context. Only those concerns consistently identified throughout the scripture as moral imperatives necessary to the authentic self-understanding of God's people can be made necessary marks of faith in the present.

3. The Bible can provide theological perspectives which focus the church's response to ethical issues. Even when basic identity and imperatives are clear within the church, its response to ethical concerns can be crippled by narrowness of theological perspective. In its diversity the Bible provides a complete range of theological viewpoints, no one of which can be called *the* biblical theology, but all of which might be made available as appropriate contexts for ethical response in a given set of circumstances. The appropriateness of any theological perspective offered in the biblical material must be judged on the basis of the ethical situation with constant attention that it does not distort the basic biblical self-understanding of the church.

This use of the Bible can best be illustrated by focusing again on the issue of hunger and poverty. If the biblical imperatives concerning the poor and the hungry are clear, it has been less clear how those imperatives are to be acted upon in the life of the church. Much will depend on the theological perspectives which focus our response. A dominant biblical theological model in the Old Testament is salvation history. The focus is on God's actions in history to redeem his people. The central event, of course, is the crossing of the sea. This exodus event becomes paradigmatic for Israel's life and faith. Stress is placed on the situations of distress in which the community constantly finds itself, and on the community's inability to deliver itself. Although God may judge his people, the community can ultimately put trust and hope in the assurance of God's deliverance. This is an extremely appropriate model for theologies founded in the suffering and oppression of the world's poor and hungry, and has been heavily used by the liberation theologies. Deliverance, redemption and salvation, effected by God's intervention against the world's hostile forces, provide the basis for hope in seemingly hopeless situations.

For a response to global hunger and poverty on the part of American middle class churches this may be a much less appropriate theological framework. Too often when these churches have used the salvation history themes they appear to place themselves in the immodest role of God's agents bringing deliverance and salvation. Thus, our aid and charity approaches to concern for hunger and poverty appear patronizing and self-congratulatory.

Alternative theological perspectives might transform this inadequate ethical response. For example, if we turned to the wisdom literature of the Old Testament we would find a stress on God as creator rather than as deliverer. Out of this grows an emphasis on preserving and enriching life within the created order and a focus on the importance of human freedom and responsibility in this task. Such a theological perspective might encourage abandonment of the rescuer mentality and impel us to work for the establishment of a more just and harmonious world order. Causes would be treated rather than symptoms. We would also be forced to place greater importance on our own role as bringers of life or death in the human order by the decisions we make. Our role in patterns that have created the suffering of world poverty and hunger would be exposed, and the church could be called to repentance for its participation.

In this use of the Bible a particular action is not dictated, but a variety of possible frameworks for action are presented. It is important not to absolutize any of these. The richness of the Bible as an ethical resource lies partly in the constant critique and corrective that a variety of theological perspectives provide in relation to one another. Our choice of biblical foundations ought to be made as carefully as our choice of ethical strategies.

4. The Bible can act as a resource for decision-making on particular issues when a clear moral imperative is not already internalized within the community. What are we to do in a given ethical situation? We have left this use until last because this has often been the entire focus of discussions on the relationship between the Bible and Christian ethics.

This use of the Bible starts with the issue that calls for decision. One comes to the Bible with an agenda already set. Here the use of the Bible becomes truly dialogic. The biblical material is placed into dialog with all of those factors defining an issue in a concrete situation in the life of the church. The amount of resource material one finds in the Bible will vary. For some issues there may be places in the scripture where that same issue is directly addressed. Material pertinent to the issue at hand may be implied in stories of biblical people and events. There may be a variety of materials and perspectives on a given question. Biblical principles such as justice may apply to the given issue. When the issue is such that it is not directly addressed or even implied at all (e.g. organ transplants) then one may be forced to rely solely on the biblical witness to general values and attitudes that might inform contemporary deciding.

It is important to exhaust the full range of the biblical canon in seeking resources for decision-making. Then the resultant biblical material may function in several different ways.

An investigation of biblical resources may reveal a polarity of positions. Responsible moral judgment cannot absolutize one or the other of these poles but must struggle for decision within the tension established in the biblical witness. For example, the Bible teaches that one is to obey God rather than man when human demands seem in conflict with God's will (see the stories of Daniel), but it also teaches obedience to civil authorities as these offices are ordained by God (Romans 13). One can responsibly reach ethical decisions in this area by taking both poles of this tension seriously. The Bible then serves to identify the creative tension in which decision-making must take place. The tension may be an unequal one. Christians in revolutionary situations have had to struggle with the question of violence. The overwhelming witness of the scripture is against violence as a normal means to moral ends. Jesus' restraint of Peter in Gethsemane in favor of willingly going to his own death has often been cited as an example. But the Bible also witnesses to God's wrath against the wicked, and those in the biblical communities are sometimes called upon to stand physically against evil. Those who must struggle with this question must take account of the preponderant emphasis on one pole of this tension, and carefully weigh the biblical witness to circumstances under which the other pole might be enjoined. A final decision can only be one taken in the risk of faith within the tension of the biblical witness.

A careful search of biblical materials may uncover a whole range of options or perspectives. In the area of sexual ethics one must reckon with the widest divergence of material. Genesis 1 and 2 affirm the created goodness and harmony of the male-female relationship. Proverbs warns of the dangerous snares of sexual enticement. Sexual attraction to one's wife is in keeping with wisdom, but the lure of the harlot is folly. The Song of Songs is a book of love songs extolling the joys of love and sexual relationship. It does not speak of marriage or societal norms. Paul in 1 Corinthians 7 seems to regard marriage as better than unbridled passion, but recommends celibacy as the best course. 1 Timothy 2:12ff. regards women as subordinate as a result of being the first transgressor, and implies that the value of sexual relationship is only in child-bearing for the redemption of the woman. Certainly no single view of human sexuality shows through here, and it would be sheer folly to declare one of these as *the* biblical view. Those who approach the Bible for guidance on questions of sexual ethics must take all of these viewpoints into account. It will be especially important to investigate the way in which each is responding to the unique context of its own time. The biblical materials then become resources for helping to clarify the options and priorities in our own concrete situation.

Finally the ethical issue at hand may simply not be addressed by the biblical material. Issues such as organ transplants, genetic experimentation, and abortion are all issues which deal with biological data not known or in any way dealt with in the biblical material. Yet even here the Bible may play a role in decision-making. An investigation of biblical resources may serve to set the boundaries within which moral inquiry takes place. Surely the biblical stress on the sanctity of human life and on the quality of human existence form boundaries within which these issues must be decided even if the specific issues themselves are not mentioned. This moral framework already begins to limit the decisions that might be taken.

In using the Bible as a resource for decision-making it is important to emphasize that the Bible can never take the burden of decision off the decision-maker. Biblical material may provide a focus in the process of decision-making, but in those areas where there is not a direct and clear moral imperative, biblical warrants will never be completely sufficient as the basis for moral decision. As noted earlier they must function dialogically with other non-biblical sources of moral insight. Our previous discussion of biblical authority noted that in this more relational use of scripture, insights from the biblical material function as the primary sources for Christian ethical reflection but are not self-sufficient.

Analogy is a word often used in connection with the use of the Bible in decision-making. Certainly any use of the Bible for this purpose involves some analogy-making. To judge that any particular biblical materials speak to a given issue is to make a kind of analogy. One should, however, avoid arguing that one searches the scripture for a situation fully analogous to some modern situation and then follows the moral remedy suggested there. Seldom will any biblical context be fully analogous to any modern situation. But even if one supposed that it were, it would be a mistake to assume that any one biblical analogy exhausts the biblical resources related to an issue. We would prefer to speak of putting biblical materials and modern situations into dialog rather than into analogies.

Finally, we must say one last word on the matter of control in using the Bible for decision-making. We have noted that fundamental to the scripture is the insight that being is inseparable from doing. The basic control, when the church attempts to decide what it should do, is its own understanding of what it has been called to be. The biblically based identity of the church as the people of God forms the constant reference point for any ethical decision on a particular issue. A decision that violates that basic identity is suspect even though it might be claiming biblical warrants. In fact, the church has often tended to place the cart before the horse by deciding immediately on ethical issues without taking adequate measure of the biblical resources available to assist in decision-making. Making decisions apart from the formation of basic Christian character is hollow and meaningless. The Bible must relate to both of these realities if it is to be truly available as a resource for the Christian moral life.

7 bible and ethics in the life of the church

In the preceding chapters we have attempted to describe the relationship of the Bible to Christian ethics by considering our subject in the total framework of the Christian moral life. In this brief chapter we shall sketch an overview of the ground we have covered and suggest some implications of our work for the life of the church.

An Overview

In the diagram that follows we have tried to represent schematically several interactive dichotomies which we have found operating in the Christian moral life. The arrows are intended to represent a constant interaction between the two sides of the diagram. These categories are not separated from one another in any absolute sense. They constantly influence and affect one another. Occasionally the boundary is difficult to determine, and occasionally the two poles stand in some tension with one another. They are useful, however, in describing the dichotomies within which the Christian moral life is dynamically lived.

195

THE CHRISTIAN MORAL LIFE

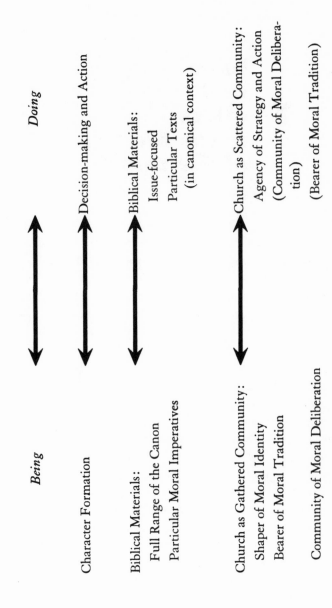

Being		*Doing*
Character Formation	↕	Decision-making and Action
Biblical Materials: Full Range of the Canon Particular Moral Imperatives	↕	Biblical Materials: Issue-focused Particular Texts (in canonical context)
Church as Gathered Community: Shaper of Moral Identity Bearer of Moral Tradition Community of Moral Deliberation	↕	Church as Scattered Community: Agency of Strategy and Action (Community of Moral Delibera- tion) (Bearer of Moral Tradition)

One side of the diagram is designated as aspects of the ethics of being. The focus is on those factors that contribute to Christian moral identity. In seeking to understand the task of Christian ethics in this area we have centered on the formation of moral character. Here we are dealing with the self and the communities which form the basic perception, dispositions and intentions of the self. The shaping of the moral agent is as crucial for ethics as the making of moral decisions. The Bible's role becomes centrally important when we begin to speak about the formation of *Christian* moral character. We have seen that the Bible is the prime source of the self-conscious identity of the Christian community. In this dimension of the moral life it is the full range of the biblical canon that becomes applicable. Materials that do not explicitly address moral concerns may still serve to shape beliefs, values and attitudes that are fundamental to the Christian community. Particular texts may come into play here in terms of clear moral imperatives, witnessed consistently throughout the canon, that are to be incorporated into the basic character of all Christians. The church is the necessary community context in which this use of the Bible in the formation of Christian character takes place. Basically the church as *gathered* community carries out this task since its nature requires the steady, ongoing nurture of the Christian community. We discussed the church's role as shaper of moral identity, bearer of moral tradition, and community of moral deliberation in a previous chapter.

The other side of the diagram lists elements generally related to the ethics of doing. This is the most common focus of ethical discussion since it deals with decision-making and action related to particular issues. The Bible's role in this aspect of the moral life is one of response to the necessity for making a decision on a given issue. Here particular texts relating to the specific area of moral concern are consulted. The interaction stressed by our diagram reminds us that these particular texts should be understood in their total canonical context as a control against distortion of the biblical witness. The results of this issue-oriented consulting of the Bible will vary widely. We saw in the previous chapter that there is no single way in which biblical materials function in relation to ethical decision-making and action. When we think of the church as it relates to this side of the ethical task, we generally think of the church as the scattered community at work in its mission and witness to the world. Especially since social ethics has occupied so much attention in the American setting, we are accustomed to seeing the church's role here as mainly an agent of strategy and action. Again the dynamic interrelationship indicated by the arrows on the diagram suggests that the church could not function in its witness to society apart from moral deliberation within its ranks which draws on the beliefs, values and attitudes shaped there in relation to the biblical witness. Further, if the church takes its distinctive identity into the world in decision and action, then even as the scattered community the church serves as bearer of and witness to a particular moral tradition.

The diagram may help to visualize the interaction of Bible and ethics in the Christian moral life, but it is well to remember that the Bible itself, as we noted in the previous chapter, allows no final division between being and doing in the life of faith.

Implications for the Church

The rejoining of biblical resources with ethical concerns along the lines we have suggested in the preceding chapters has implications for the church both in its gathered life and in its scattered life.

1. The various functions of the church in its life as a gathered community are not usually considered as primary arenas for the church's ethical life. In the common view, ethics refers to the church's dealing with issues out in the world. Elements of church life, such as preaching, liturgy, Christian education, and Christian nurture, are often understood to relate mainly to personal faith and congregational community. These are considered essential to the life of the church while ethical concerns are held separate and considered optional, available to those in the congregation who are more "socially concerned." The Bible is understood by most to be intimately tied to these aspects of gathered church life, and for that reason is seldom taken seriously as a resource for the church's ethical life.

To be sure, in most churches there are occasions when ethical issues find their way into the internal life of the church. An occasional "prophetic sermon" is preached. The liturgy may include a powerful sending forth to service and action. The Christian education program may include a series of topical issues of the day. But the fundamental dynamic in all of these activities is that ethics is to be found "out there." These occasional activities seem to function as pep talks encouraging us to get back out there where ethics is done.

We believe that a clear understanding of the Bible's role in the Christian moral life implies that *the gathered life of the church is as fundamentally ethical in nature as the scattered life of the church*. In the shaping of moral character the Bible has its greatest influence on the Christian moral life, and in the internal life of the gathered community the clearest opportunities for the development of moral character occur.

The internal life of congregations has too often become an end in itself. To see the activities of the gathered community as the development of moral agents called to responsible life as agents of reconciliation in a broken world would provide purpose to many congregations that have turned in upon themselves. Preaching, liturgy, Christian education, and Christian nurture all become activities crucial to the moral life, and it is the Bible that provides the foundation for them all. It is only in relation to the biblical witness that these activities serve to establish anew the basic identity of the church as the faithful community of the people of God. Each of these elements in the gathered life of the church would serve to communicate basic beliefs, values and attitudes which transcend individual persons and congregations. To draw out the moral dimensions of the church's internal life would heighten awareness of membership in the whole body of those whose character and conduct are shaped by a common biblical faith.

To unite biblical resources with ethical concerns in the gathered life of the church is to take up the long range task of development and nurture. The church's moral responsibility is not limited to the immediate response to crisis issues. If basic biblical understandings are not incorporated by Christians before a moral and ethical crisis arises then biblical resources are unlikely to play any significant role.

If the church wishes to relate its biblical heritage to its ethical concerns, every aspect of its life must be seen as a part of this task. Worship is crucial because it is the continual medium for those basic symbols, stories, images, rituals, and traditions, founded in the biblical tradition that carry the meaning of the faith formative of Christian character. Worship has both direct and indirect impact upon the "seeing" so central to the Christian moral life. Worship and ethics are of a piece. Yet few worship experiences are planned with the following among the serious shaping questions: What in composing the worship experience would contribute to the shaping of Christian character and conduct? What, as best we can judge, will be the outcome for Christian moral development of worship planned in this particular manner and conducted with these particular materials? These ought not be the only questions in the planning of worship, of course. The meaning of worship is more than its meaning for the moral life but it cannot be less. Thus the worship life of the congregation ought in part to be governed in a deliberate manner by the considerations central to the Christian moral life.

The task of Christian education is equally crucial. It is often limited to children with little offered for adults of any serious nature. This may well be because Christian education is not seen as serving any serious purpose for adults, and yet study and reflection on our biblical and theological resources is fundamental for equipping church people for their role as moral agents. Ironically, it is often those most anxious to make the church "relevant" who ignore this basic need for long-term training and grounding in the church's own moral resources. Although children's education is important preparation, it is only with mature adulthood that the full witness of the scripture can be grasped and understood. To sacrifice all programs for the long-term development of Christian moral character in favor of immediate activity in the world is ultimately to render the church ineffective in dealing with critical concerns.

2. As mentioned, the church's life as a scattered community encountering the world has usually been regarded as the primary locus for Christian ethical concerns. The need for ethical decision and action arises as issues present themselves from the wider social context and demand Christian response. Many in the church have labored to undertake this response seriously. Yet, as we have noted previously, it is increasingly difficult to distinguish the church's response from that of many secular groups. Christians often fail to bring with them any self-conscious understand-

ing of their own identity as the church when they tackle ethical questions. Christians who are deeply concerned with moral matters nevertheless show little awareness of particular moral resources within their own faith tradition, particularly the Bible.

Our understanding of the Bible's relationship to Christian character and conduct implies that *the scattered life of the church is as fundamentally biblical in its foundation as the gathered life of the church.* It is in the Bible that what is commonly called "Christian social action" finds its roots. The church interacts with society on ethical issues not out of some pious "do-goodism" or out of a vague humanism, but out of a biblical calling to work as agents of confrontation, witness, and reconciliation in a broken world. The church's ethical involvement finds an adequate rationale only as it relates to biblical understandings of God's will.

The results of relating biblical understandings to ethical concerns is nowhere seen more clearly than in some of the powerful theologies of liberation coming out of the Third World.[1] On the one hand, these theologies grow out of the involvement of the church in the actual struggles and sufferings of persons in need of liberation. They are founded in the church's practical engagement. On the other hand they have drawn deeply on biblical understandings in their seeking after God's will for his people in these situations. Christian conduct is grounded in and empowered by the biblical witness.

These theologies of liberation indicate that the positioning of the church in the midst of moral struggles enables the biblical word to be fully heard and its implications to be fully appropriated. Inability to hear God's word is often the failure of the church to rightly situate itself in the brokenness of the world it is sent to reconcile. Only in such a context is it really possible to discover the moral address of the scripture. For example, the Bible's radical imperative to identify with and care for the dispossessed cannot really be understood by a middle-class suburban congregation apart from the effort and risk to become involved with the hungry, the poor, or the oppressed. When the church is truly scattered in the world and shares its brokenness it is impelled back to its basic biblical foundation to see with new eyes. A new climate for the reception of God's word is created and a new vision is born. In turn, a new urgency is brought to the work of the gathered community in equipping the church for its moral task. The gathered community and the scattered community are now seen as complementary in relation to the Christian moral life. Neither can function with integrity apart from the other, and in the biblical witness, seen with new clarity, their unity is found.

In practical terms this means that those in the church who are concerned with ethical issues must take worship, study, and reflection much more seriously as essential to the empowerment of the church's moral witness. It means that decisions and actions cannot be taken hastily apart from some clear assessment of the particular resources that the church might bring to an issue. This does not mean that the church is rendered incapable of timely response. It simply suggests that those who are involved with ethical issues in the wider social context must also be concerned and involved with the long-term task of shaping moral perceptions, dispositions and intentions in the church, so that Christians might stand ready for meaningful and timely response.

Another task for which the church is scattered in the world is evangelism, the church's witness to a particular faith perspective. In recent times the ethical activists and those concerned with evangelism have stood, for the most part, in separate camps within the church. The understanding of the Christian moral life which we have developed in the preceding chapters makes clear that this is a false division. If Christian moral activity is properly rooted in biblical faith then the church is constantly witnessing to that particular faith as it is at work in the world. Moral involvement and evangelical witness in the world become joined. The church's witness to the meaning of its own faith is then properly joined to its concern for reconciliation in a broken world, and both are grounded in the biblical witness. Salvation then becomes a term that encompasses both issues of faith and issues of ethical concern for the fullness of human life.[2]

* * * * *

Although we began this volume by noting that the community of faith has always regarded the Bible as the charter document of the Christian moral life, we observed that the pattern in our time has too often been one of divergence between our biblical resources and our moral concerns.

It is our hope that the pattern might become one of reunion for the strengthening of the church's witness in a time when the need for inspiration and guidance in shaping our lives is urgent. Crises of basic belief and compelling vision run deep. Commitments worthy of life and death dedication elude the lives of most. Moral and ethical issues are confronted with unabating frequency and growing complexity.

To make the connections between Bible and ethics in the Christian life will not of itself meet the faith crises, evoke worthy commitments, or resolve pressing moral issues. It can help to provide a foundation for those tasks. If this book can, even in a small way, assist in linking the Christian's moral struggle with the church's rich fund of biblical resources, it will have served its purpose well.

notes

Introduction

1. Brevard Childs, *Biblical Theology in Crisis* (Philadelphia: Westminster, 1970) 124.

1

The Divergence of Biblical Studies and Christian Ethics

1. James M. Gustafson, "Christian Ethics," in Paul Ramsey, ed., *Religion* (Englewood Cliffs: Prentice-Hall, 1965) 337.

2. Charles Curran, "Dialogue with the Scriptures: The Role and Function of the Scriptures in Moral Theology," in *Catholic Moral in Dialogue* (Notre Dame: Fides, 1972) 24.

3. Leander E. Keck and James E. Sellers, "Theological Ethics in an American Crisis: A Case Study," *Interpretation,* 24, (1970), 469-470.

4. Curran, 24.

5. John Howard Yoder, *The Politics of Jesus* (Grand Rapids: Eerdmans, 1972) 13-14.

6. One invitation we shall take up in the next chapter is C. Freeman Sleeper's "Ethics as a Context for Biblical Interpretation" in *Interpretation,* 22 (1968), 443-460. Leander Keck, in another ar-

ticle—"On the Ethos of Early Christians," *Journal of the American Academy of Religion* (Vol. XLII, No. 3, September 1974)—suggests that theological reflection in the New Testament might well have emerged "from the penetration of ethical issues in order to find appropriate criteria for dealing with the actual lives of early Christians, a penetration prompted by the ongoing interaction of gospel and ethos" (pp. 451-452). Keck's point is "that the relation of theology and ethics in the New Testament might be reversed" (p. 451) so that in actual fact it might have been moral deliberation that occasioned theological articulation, rather than ethics appearing as an appendage or even the "practical application" of the community's already formulated theology.

7. A full survey is clearly beyond the scope of these pages. We limit ourselves to the main lines of development in each of the two disciplines.

8. Gustafson, 287.

9. *Ibid.*

10. *Ibid.*, 311-312.

11. The terms are Gustafson's from the above-cited essay, upon which we continue to rely heavily.

12. Two influential American ethicists which represent this change are H. Richard Niebuhr and Paul Lehmann. It is striking that in the ethics of Niebuhr few pages are given to discussion of the moral instruction portions of the Bible and for Lehmann none at all. Yet for both the overriding importance of the Bible is clear. See H. Richard Niebuhr, *The Responsible Self*, New York: Harper and Row, 1963; and Paul Lehmann, *Ethics in a Christian Context*, New York: Harper and Row, 1963.

13. Gustafson, 317.

14. *Ibid.*

15. Karl Barth, *The Humanity of God*, trans. Thomas Weiser, (Richmond: John Knox, 1963) 86. Cited in Gene Outka, *Agape: An Ethical Analysis* (New Haven: Yale University Press, 1972) 231.

16. Curran, 26.

17. There are historical reasons for this which we shall not entertain here. See Curran, 25-27.

18. Perhaps the most influential of the early works was that of Rudolf Schnackenburg, *The Moral Teaching of the New Testament* (New York: Herder and Herder, 1965). The German original was published in 1954.

19. See Bernard Häring, C.SS.R., *The Law of Christ* (3 volumes, Westminster, MD.: Newman, 1961, 1963, 1966).

20. Curran, 53.

21. Gustafson, 287.

22. Gustafson as cited above, opening page of this chapter.

23. See e.g., Carl F. H. Henry, *Christian Personal Ethics* (Grand Rapids: Eerdmans, 1957).

24. Sydney Ahlstrom in *A Religious History of the American People* (New Haven: Yale University Press, 1972) 782, distinguishes two groups in American Liberalism which he calls "Evangelical Liberalism" and "Modernistic Liberalism." The former included the Social Gospel movement while the latter included this more detached attempt at an objective and scholarly liberal approach to the Bible.

25. The development, interests and collapse of this "biblical theology movement" has been carefully documented in Brevard Childs, *Biblical Theology in Crisis*, Philadelphia: Westminster, 1970.

26. *Ibid.*, 21.

27. *Eschatology and Ethics in the Teaching of Jesus* (New York: Harper, 1939); "The Basis of Christian Ethics in the New Testament," *Journal of Religious Thought* 15 (1957), 141-142; *Kerygma, Eschatology, and Social Ethics* (Philadelphia: Fortress, 1966).

28. C. H. Dodd, *Gospel and Law* (New York: Columbia University Press, 1951), and "The Ethics of the New Testament," *Moral Principles of Action*, edited by Ruth Nanda Anshen (New York: Harper, 1952) 543-558. T. W. Manson, *Ethics and the Gospel* (New York: Scribner's, 1960). R. Schnackenburg, *The Moral Teaching of the New Testament* (New York: Herder and Herder, 1965) is the English translation of the 1954 German edition which represented the culmination of work on New Testament

ethics which appeared in numerous articles through the fifties. Paul Minear, one of the key participants in the biblical theology movement, turned his attention toward biblical ethics after the collapse of the new biblical theology with *Commands of Christ: Authority and Implications* (Nashville: Abingdon, 1972).

29. Childs, 59.

30. *Ibid.*, 60.

31. "Biblical Theology, Contemporary," *Interpreter's Dictionary of the Bible,* (Vol. 1, Nashville: Abingdon, 1962) 418ff.

32. New York: Harper, 1961.

33. (Vol. 2, Nashville: Abingdon, 1962) 1153-1161. This article is a summary of his longer German work *Das Ethos des Alten Testaments* (Berlin: A. Töpfelmann, 1938). Also important is the English translation of Vol. 2 of Walther Eichrodt, *Theology of the Old Testament* (Philadelphia: Westminster, 1967) which contains a section on "The Effect of Piety on Conduct (Old Testament Morality)" 316-379.

34. Baltimore: Penguin Books, 1973.

35. Philadelphia: Fortress, 1975.

36. Nashville: Abingdon, 1968.

37. *The Ethic of Jesus in the Teaching of the Church* (Nashville: Abingdon, 1961).

38. *The Corinthian Church: A Biblical Approach to Urban Culture* (Nashville: Abingdon, 1961).

39. *The Love Command in the New Testament* (Nashville: Abingdon, 1972).

40. *Tradition for Crisis: A Study in Hosea* (Richmond: John Knox, 1968).

41. Markus Barth and Verne Fletcher, *Acquittal by Resurrection* (New York: Holt, Rinehart and Winston, 1964); John Reumann and William Lazareth, *Righteousness and Society* (Philadelphia: Fortress, 1967); James Sellers and Leander Keck, "Theological Ethics in an American Crisis," *Interpretation,* 24 (1970), 456-481.

42. "Biblical Theology's Role in Decision-Making," *Biblical Theology in Crisis* (Philadelphia: Westminster, 1970), 123-138.

43. *Decision-Making and the Bible* (Valley Forge: Judson, 1975).

44. Jürgen Moltmann, "Christian Theology Today," *New World Outlook*, 62 (1972), 483-490.

45. See James D. Smart, *The Strange Silence of the Bible in the Church* (Philadelphia: Westminster, 1970) and more recently Elizabeth Achtemeier, *The Old Testament and Proclamation of the Gospel* (Philadelphia: Westminster, 1973).

2

Relating the Bible and Christian Ethics: Recent Efforts

1. New York: Harper and Row, 1968.

2. *Interpretation*, 24, (1970) 430-455. Reprinted in James M. Gustafson, *Theology and Christian Ethics* (Philadelphia: Pilgrim, 1974).

3. *Ibid.*, 439.

4. *Ibid.*, 442.

5. *Ibid.*, 444.

6. *Ibid.*

7. James Gustafson, *The Church as Moral Decision-Maker* (Philadelphia: Pilgrim, 1970).

8. Gustafson, "The Place of Scripture," *Interpretation*, 433.

9. *Ibid.*, 455.

10. James Gustafson, "Christian Ethics," in Paul Ramsey, ed., *Religion* (Englewood Cliffs, N.J.: Prentice-Hall, 1965), 337.

11. James M. Gustafson, *Theology and Christian Ethics,* 148.

12. *Ibid.*, 159.

13. Edward LeRoy Long Jr., "The Use of the Bible in Christian Ethics," *Interpretation* 19 (1965), 149.

14. *Ibid.*, 153.

15. *Ibid.*, 154-158.

16. *Ibid.*, 158-162.

17. See Edward LeRoy Long Jr., *A Survey of Christian Ethics* (New York and London: Oxford University Press, 1967) 310-314.

18. The discussion here draws on the article by Curran cited in the previous chapter, "Dialogue with the Scriptures: The Role and Function of the Scriptures in Moral Theology."

19. *Ibid.*, 37-47.

20. *Ibid.*, 54.

21. *Ibid.*

22. *Ibid.*

23. *Ibid.* Curran's remark here is made about methodology as a whole in Christian ethics and not only that portion pertaining to the use of the Bible. But because it holds equally well for that we cite it here.

24. H. Edward Everding and Dana Wilbanks, "A Functional Methodology for Relating Biblical Studies and Contemporary Ethics" (An unpublished paper for the American Academy of Religion Consultation on the Bible and Ethics, October, 1974) 7-14.

25. *Ibid.*, 8.

26. Everding and Wilbanks' phrase for the components integrating Bible and ethics.

27. *Ibid.*, 9.

28. *Ibid.*, 10.

29. *Ibid.*, 9-10.

30. Curran, 42.

31. Everding and Wilbanks, 10.

32. *Ibid.*, 11.

33. *Ibid.*

34. *Ibid.*

35. *Ibid.*, 13.

36. *Ibid.*, 13-14.

37. Everding and Wilbanks have published their methodology, together with case studies in book form intended for congregational use. See their *Decision-Making and the Bible* (Valley Forge, Pennsylvania: Judson, 1975).

38. Brevard S. Childs, "Biblical Theology's Role in Decision-Making," *Biblical Theology in Crisis* (Philadelphia: Westminster, 1970), 123-138.

39. *Ibid.,* 126.

40. *Ibid.,* 129.

41. *Ibid.,* 131.

42. *Ibid.,* 132.

43. Childs has more fully developed this theme in one of several chapters illustrative of his method entitled "Proverbs, Chapter 7, and a Biblical Approach to Sex," 184-200.

44. *Ibid.,* 135-136.

45. C. Freeman Sleeper, "Ethics as a Context for Biblical Interpretation," *Interpretation,* 22 (1968), 443-460. A somewhat different version of this essay was published as the first chapter in Sleeper's book, *Black Power and Christian Responsibility* (Nashville: Abingdon, 1968).

46. *Ibid.,* 445-446.

47. This quotation is from pp. 19-20 of the essay in *Black Power and Christian Responsibility.*

48. P. 451 of the *Interpretation* essay.

49. *Ibid.*

3

Understanding the Task of Christian Ethics

1. See Chap. 2, pp. 60-61.

2. Curran, 54.

3. Earlier we noted that the Roman Catholic tradition has always given an important place to the "virtues." Recent Protestant works of special significance for this subject of character in the moral life include Stanley Hauerwas' *Vision and Virtue* (Notre Dame: Fides, 1974) and *Character and the Christian Life: A Study in Theological Ethics* (San Antonio: Trinity University Press, 1975; David Bailey Harned, *Faith and Virtue* (Phila-

delphia: Pilgrim, 1973); James M. Gustafson, *Can Ethics Be Christian?* (Chicago: University of Chicago Press, 1975).

4. It is clear that our use of the term "identity" as a synonym for the particular being of a person is a broader one than its well-known use in the writings of Erik Erikson. Our use should not be confused with that focus upon a process distinctive to a particular stage of life.

   It might also be added here that our discussion of identity in no way intends to deny genetic determinants in the formation of self. But because our arena of concern is ethics, therefore an arena of choices and responses to choices, we concentrate on that formation which is the outcome of the dialog of self and society.

5. Nothing is implied here about a full identification of the self's interests and values with those of the self's communities. That may occur, of course, but it is not a logical necessity of the theory of self and society presented in this book. In fact, we would argue as strongly as possible against the nurture of such identification. It is, among other things, idolatrous. The comment of Ronald V. Sampson is instructive:

   > Unless an individual's sense of identity and purpose are securely located in a metaphysic which transcends the claims of particularist groups, he will be very prone to derive his sense of significance from the values of the group or groups with which he identifies himself. Accordingly any threat to those groups will be experienced as a threat to the stability of the individual ego identifying with them.

   (From: Ronald V. Sampson, *The Psychology of Power* [New York: Pantheon Books, 1966], 203).
   In light of our presentation it need only be added that the kind of metaphysic of which Sampson speaks is itself socially mediated.

6. See the discussion of "faith" in the presentation of the work of Everding and Wilbanks in Chap. 2, pp. 62-63.

7. The designation of these three areas of persistent concern for ethics follows the scheme of James Gustafson in the first chapter of his book, *Christ and the Moral Life*.

8. Aristotle, *Nicomachean Ethics,* 2.1, cited from James M. Gustafson's *Can Ethics Be Christian?* 41.

9. There is an important sense in which it is misleading to speak of the "identity" or "character" of a community. The active agent that puts together the various factors into a distinctive constellation is the person, the individual self. Thus in a strict sense only the "I" can be described as having an identity or character. To speak of "the self" of a community or a people, society or a nation, is to speak of something different. It remains meaningful and indeed essential to talk of *corporate* identity or character, however, and indicate by that those powerful shared traits and qualities of being in the common life that deeply affect the distinctive personalities of individuals.

10. Karl Barth, *Church Dogmatics* III/4 (Edinburgh: T. and T. Clark, 1961), trans. by A. T. Mackay, *et al., passim.*

11. Childs, 129. The earlier reference was made in Chap. 2, p. 68.

12. The suggestion is that of Edward LeRoy Long Jr. in his *A Survey of Christian Ethics,* "A Prolegomena to Comprehensive Complementarity," 310ff.

13. William Stringfellow, *An Ethic for Christians and Other Aliens in a Strange Land* (Waco, Texas: Word Books, 1973), 13.

14. Much of the thrust of this chapter is captured in the musings of Undersecretary of State Chester Bowles recorded a month after the Bay of Pigs incident.

> The question which concerns me most about this new Administration is whether it lacks a genuine sense of conviction about what is right and what is wrong. I realize in posing the question I am raising an extremely serious point. Nevertheless I feel it must be faced.
>
> Anyone in public life who has strong convictions about the rights and wrongs of public morality, both domestic and international, has a very great advantage in times of strain, since his instincts on what to do are clear and immediate. Lacking such a framework of moral conviction or sense of what is right and what is wrong, he is forced to lean almost entirely upon his mental processes; he adds up the plusses and minuses of any question and comes up with a conclu-

sion. Under normal conditions, when he is not tired or frustrated, this pragmatic approach should successfully bring him out on the right side of the question.

What worries me are the conclusions that such an individual may reach when he is tired, angry, frustrated, or emotionally affected. The Cuban fiasco demonstrates how far astray a man as brilliant and well intentioned as Kennedy can go who lacks a basic moral reference point.

Cited from David Halberstam, *The Best and the Brightest* (Greenwich, Connecticut: Fawcett Publications, 1972), 88.

4
The Church as a Community Context

1. There are some notable exceptions of high quality, however: James M. Gustafson, *The Church as Moral Decision-Maker* (Philadelphia: Pilgrim, 1970); David Bailey Harned, *Faith and Virtue* (Philadelphia: Pilgrim, 1973); Paul Lehmann, *Ethics in a Christian Context* (New York: Harper & Row, 1963); James B. Nelson, *Moral Nexus: Ethics of Christian Identity and Community* (Philadelphia: Westminster, 1973).

2. The discussion here is indebted to David H. Kelsey's *The Use of Scripture in Recent Theology* (Philadelphia: Fortress, 1975) 89ff. Readers who wish to explore the general subject of the relationship of church, scripture and tradition may profitably consult: Yves M.-J. Congar, O.P., *Tradition and Traditions* (New York: Macmillan, 1967); and P. C. Rodger and Lukas Vischer, eds., *The Fourth World Conference on Faith and Order* (New York: Association, 1964).

3. Nelson, 96.

4. Kelsey, 95.

5. *Ibid.,* 96.

6. Gustafson, *The Church as Moral Decision-Maker,* 83ff.

7. Henry David Aiken, "The Levels of Moral Discourse," *Reason and Conduct* (New York: Knopf, 1962) 65ff.

8. Paul Ramsey's *Who Speaks for the Church?* (Nashville: Abingdon, 1967), and the debate it provoked are instructive here. Part III, "The Implementation of Ethical Decisions," of Edward LeRoy Long Jr.'s *A Survey of Christian Ethics* provides a helpful typology.

5

Biblical Authority and Non-Biblical Sources

1. A most helpful discussion of these matters is found in David H. Kelsey, *The Uses of Scripture in Recent Theology* (Philadelphia: Fortress, 1975) 89ff.

2. James Gustafson, "Introduction," H. Richard Niebuhr, *The Responsible Self* (New York: Harper and Row, 1963), 22.

3. James Barr, *The Bible in the Modern World* (New York: Harper and Row, 1973) 23.

4. *Ibid.,* 13.

5. James Gustafson, "Introduction," in Niebuhr, *The Responsible Self,* 22.

6. See Larry Rasmussen, "Thinking Through the Unthinkable: Triage and Lifeboat Ethics," *Hunger in the Global Community* (Washington: Center for the Study of Power and Peace, 1975).

7. Allen Dale Verhey, *The Use of Scripture in Moral Discourse: A Case Study of Walter Rauschenbusch.* Unpublished dissertation (Yale University, 1975), 1-8.

6

Making Biblical Resources Available

1. See Chap. 1 n. 45.

2. Roy Sano has developed this text in relation to an ethnic theology in an unpublished address, "A Liberating and Unmeltable White Ethnicity," available from the Asian Center for Theology and Strategies, Mills College, Oakland, California.

3. *Biblical Theology in Crisis,* 99. Much of this discussion of canon is indebted to Childs' work in this area. Readers wishing a fuller discussion should consult this book at length.

4. Paul Lehmann, *Ethics in a Christian Context* (New York: Harper and Row, 1963) briefly acknowledges the importance of Old Testament roots (p. 26) and cites the Reformation principle of *Tota Scriptura est verbum dei* (The Scripture as a whole is the Word of God, p. 30), but entitles his section on biblical resources "Christian Ethics and New Testament Ethics" (p. 26).

5. Childs, 105.

6. *Ibid.,* 195f. Childs notes a number of negative controls on looking for similarity of subject matter.

7. See pp. 179-182 above.

7

Bible and Ethics in the Life of the Church

1. A representative and widely respected example in Gustavo Gutierrez, *A Theology of Liberation* (Maryknoll, N.Y.: Orbis, 1973).

2. This discussion seems to be underway in the global Christian community as evidenced by the landmark meeting of the Commission on World Mission and Evangelism in Bangkok on the theme Salvation Today. This discussion should receive more attention within the American churches. A wide array of documents related to the Bangkok meeting are available from the World Council of Churches.

bibliography

Achtemeier, Elizabeth. *The Old Testament and Proclamation of the Gospel*. Philadelphia: Westminster Press, 1973.

Aiken, Henry David. "The Levels of Moral Discourse," *Reason and Conduct*. New York: Knopf, 1962, 65ff.

Baird, William. *The Corinthian Church: A Biblical Approach to Urban Culture*. Nashville: Abingdon Press, 1961.

Barr, James. *The Bible in the Modern World*. New York: Harper and Row, 1973.

Barth, Karl. *Church Dogmatics*. Translated by A. T. Mackay, *et al.* Vol. III, Pt. 4. Edinburgh: T. and T. Clark, 1961.

Barth, Karl. *The Humanity of God*. Translated by Thomas Weiser Richmond: John Knox Press, 1963.

Barth, Markus, and Fletcher, Verne. *Acquittal by Resurrection*. New York: Holt, Rinehart and Winston, 1964.

Breuggeman, Walter. *Tradition for Crisis: A Study in Hosea*. Richmond: John Knox Press, 1968.

Childs, Brevard S. *Biblical Theology in Crisis*. Philadelphia: Westminster Press, 1970.

Curran, Charles E. "Dialogue with the Scriptures: The Role and Function of the Scriptures in Moral Theology," *Catholic Moral Theology in Dialogue*. Notre Dame, Ind.: Fides Publishers, 1972, 24-64.

Dodd, C. H. "The Ethics of the New Testament," *Moral Principles of Action*. Edited by Ruth Nanda Anshen. New York: Harper and Brothers, 1952, 543-558.

Dodd, C. H. *Gospel and Law*. New York: Columbia University Press, 1951.

Eichrodt, Walther, "The Effect of Piety on Conduct (Old Testament morality)," *Theology of the Old Testament*. Translated by J. A. Baker. Vol. II. Philadelphia: Westminster Press, 1967, 316-379.

Everding, H. Edward, and Wilbanks, Dana M. *Decision-Making and the Bible*. Valley Forge: Judson Press, 1975.

Everding, H. Edward, and Wilbanks, Dana M. "A Functional Methodology for Relating Biblical Studies and Contemporary Ethics." Unpublished paper for the American Academy of Religion Consultation on the Bible and Ethics, October, 1974.

Furnish, Victor. *The Love Command in the New Testament*. Nashville: Abingdon Press, 1972.

Furnish, Victor. *Theology and Ethics in Paul*. Nashville: Abingdon Press, 1968.

Gustafson, James M. *Can Ethics Be Christian?* Chicago: University of Chicago Press, 1975.

Gustafson, James M. *Christ and the Moral Life*. New York: Harper and Row, 1968.

Gustafson, James M. "Christian Ethics," *Religion*. Edited by Paul Ramsey. Englewood Cliffs, N.J.: Prentice-Hall, Inc., 1965, 285-354.

Gustafson, James M. *The Church as Moral Decision-Maker*. Philadelphia: Pilgrim Press, 1970.

Gustafson, James M. "Introduction," *The Responsible Self* by H. Richard Niebuhr. New York: Harper and Row, 1963, 6-41.

Gustafson, James M. "The Place of Scripture in Christian Ethics: A Methodological Study, *Interpretation,* XXIV (October, 1970), 430-455.

Gustafson, James M. *Theology and Christian Ethics.* Philadelphia: Pilgrim Press, 1974.

Gutierrez, Gustavo. *A Theology of Liberation.* Maryknoll, N.Y.: Orbis Books, 1973.

Häring, Bernard. *The Law of Christ.* 3 vols. Westminster, Md.: The Newman Press, 1961, 1963, 1966.

Harned, David Bailey. *Faith and Virtue.* Philadelphia: Pilgrim Press, 1973.

Hauerwas, Stanley. *Character and the Christian Life: A Study in Theological Ethics.* San Antonio: Trinity University Press, 1975.

Hauerwas, Stanley. *Vision and Virtue.* Notre Dame: Fides Publishers, 1974.

Hempel, J. "Ethics in the Old Testament," *Interpreter's Dictionary of the Bible.* Vol. II. Nashville: Abingdon Press, 1962, 153-161.

Hempel, J. *Das Ethos des Alten Testaments.* Berlin: A. Töpelmann, 1938.

Henry, Carl F. H. *Christian Personal Ethics.* Grand Rapids: Wm. B. Eerdmans Publishing Co., 1957.

Houlden, J. L. *Ethics and the New Testament.* Baltimore: Penguin Books, 1973.

Keck, Leander E. "On the Ethos of Early Christians," *Journal of the American Academy of Religion.* Vol. XLII, No. 3 (September, 1974), 435-452.

Keck, Leander E., and Sellers, James E. "Theological Ethics in an American Crisis: A Case Study," *Interpretation,* XXIV (October, 1970), 456-481.

Kelsey, David H. *Uses of Scripture in Recent Theology.* Philadelphia: Fortress Press, 1975.

Knox, John. *The Ethics of Jesus in the Teaching of the Church.* Nashville: Abingdon Press, 1961.

Lehmann, Paul. *Ethics in a Christian Context.* New York: Harper and Row, 1963.

Long, Edward LeRoy, Jr. *A Survey of Christian Ethics.* New York: Oxford University Press, 1967.

Long, Edward LeRoy, Jr., "The Use of the Bible in Christian Ethics: A Look at Basic Options," *Interpretation,* XIX (April, 1965), 149-162.

Manson, T. W. *Ethics and the Gospel.* New York: Scribner's, 1960.

Minear, Paul S. *Commands of Christ: Authority and Implications.* Nashville: Abingdon Press, 1972.

Muilenburg, James. *The Way of Israel: Biblical Faith and Ethics.* New York: Harper and Brothers, 1961.

Nelson, James B. *Moral Nexus: Ethics of Christian Identity and Community.* Philadelphia: Westminster Press, 1973.

Niebuhr, H. Richard. *The Responsible Self.* New York: Harper and Row, 1963.

Reumann, John, and Lazareth, William. *Righteousness and Society.* Philadelphia: Fortress Press, 1967.

Sanders, Jack T. *Ethics in the New Testament.* Philadelphia: Fortress Press, 1975.

Schnackenburg, Rudolf. *The Moral Teaching of the New Testament.* New York: Herder and Herder, 1965.

Sleeper, C. Freeman. *Black Power and Christian Responsibility.* Nashville: Abingdon Press, 1968.

Sleeper, C. Freeman. "Ethics as a Context for Biblical Interpretation," *Interpretation,* XXII (October, 1968), 443-460.

Smart, James D. *The Strange Silence of the Bible in the Church.* Philadelphia: Westminster Press, 1970.

Stendahl, Krister. "Biblical Theology, Contemporary," *Interpreter's Dictionary of the Bible.* Vol. I. Nashville: Abingdon Press, 1962, 418-432.

Stringfellow, William. *An Ethic for Christians and Other Aliens in a Strange Land.* Waco, Texas: Word Books, 1973.

Wilder, Amos N. "The Basis of Christian Ethics in the New Testament," *Journal of Religious Thought*. Vol. XV, No. 2 (Spring-Summer, 1958), 137-146.

Wilder, Amos N. *Eschatology and Ethics in the Teaching of Jesus*. New York: Harper, 1939.

Wilder, Amos N. *Kerygma, Eschatology, and Social Ethics*. Philadelphia: Fortress Press, 1966.

Yoder, John Howard. *The Politics of Jesus*. Grand Rapids: Eerdmans, 1972.